Testing in Pharo

Stéphane Ducasse, Guillermo Polito and Juan Pablo Sandoval

June 4, 2023

Copyright 2023 by Stéphane Ducasse, Guillermo Polito and Juan Pablo Sandoval.

The contents of this book are protected under the Creative Commons Attribution-NonCommercial-NoDerivs CC BY-NC-ND
You are free to:

　Share — copy and redistribute the material in any medium or format

The licensor cannot revoke these freedoms as long as you follow the license terms. Under the following conditions:

Attribution. — You must give appropriate credit, provide a link to the license, and indicate if changes were made. You may do so in any reasonable manner, but not in any way that suggests the licensor endorses you or your use.

NonCommercial. — You may not use the material for commercial purposes.

NoDerivatives. — If you remix, transform, or build upon the material, you may not distribute the modified material.

No additional restrictions. — You may not apply legal terms or technological measures that legally restrict others from doing anything the license permits.

https://creativecommons.org/licenses/by-nc-nd/4.0/legalcode

Any of the above conditions can be waived if you get permission from the copyright holder. Nothing in this license impairs or restricts the author's moral rights.

Keepers of the lighthouse
Édition : BoD - Books on Demand, info@bod.fr
Impression : BoD – Books on Demand,
In de Tarpen 42, Norderstedt (Allemagne)
Impression à la demande
ISBN : 978-2-3224-8114-9
Dépôt légal : Juin 2023
Layout and typography based on the sbabook LaTeX class by Damien Pollet.

Contents

1 Introduction — 1
1.1 Outline — 1
1.2 About SUnit — 2
1.3 About typographic conventions — 2
1.4 About this book — 3
1.5 Getting started — 3

2 Two minutes of theory — 5
2.1 Automated tests — 5
2.2 Why testing is important — 6
2.3 What makes a good test? — 7
2.4 A piece of advice on testing — 8
2.5 Pharo testing rules as a conclusion — 10

3 SUnit by example — 11
3.1 Step 1: Create the test class — 11
3.2 Step 2: A first test — 12
3.3 Step 3: Run the tests — 12
3.4 Step 4: Another test — 13
3.5 Step 5: Factoring out context — 14
3.6 Step 6: Initialize the test context — 14
3.7 Step 7: Debugging a test — 15
3.8 Step 8: Interpret the results — 16
3.9 Conclusion — 16

4 Extreme Test-Driven Development by Example — 17
4.1 A simple and powerful principle — 17
4.2 Studying an example — 18
4.3 Before executing a test — 18
4.4 Executing a test to define missing methods — 19
4.5 Stepping back: Supporting the programmer flow — 23
4.6 One cycle — 24
4.7 Why XTDD is powerful? — 24

i

5 SUnit: The framework — 27
- 5.1 Understanding the framework — 27
- 5.2 During test execution — 27
- 5.3 The framework in a nutshell — 28
- 5.4 Test states — 30
- 5.5 Glossary — 31
- 5.6 Chapter summary — 32

6 A little cookbook — 33
- 6.1 Testing comments — 33
- 6.2 Parameterized tests — 34
- 6.3 Matrix: a more advanced case — 35
- 6.4 Classes vs. objects as parameters — 36
- 6.5 Other assertions — 37
- 6.6 Running tests — 38
- 6.7 Advanced features of SUnit — 39
- 6.8 Test resources — 40
- 6.9 Customising tests: Examples as tests — 43
- 6.10 Inheriting TestCase — 43
- 6.11 Conclusion — 44

7 SUnit implementation — 45
- 7.1 Running one test — 45
- 7.2 Running a TestSuite — 47

8 UI testing — 49
- 8.1 Testing Spec — 49
- 8.2 Spec user perspective — 50
- 8.3 Example — 51
- 8.4 Spec user test 2: Tree selection — 52
- 8.5 Spec user test 3: triggering the button action — 52
- 8.6 Spec user test 4: Not editable text presenter — 53
- 8.7 Spec user test 5: the window is built correctly — 53
- 8.8 Known limitations and conclusion — 53

9 Testing web applications with Parasol — 55
- 9.1 Getting started — 55
- 9.2 First steps with Selenium — 57
- 9.3 Locating elements with Parasol: The basics — 59
- 9.4 Finding elements using XPath — 61
- 9.5 Finding multiple elements — 62
- 9.6 Interacting with the elements — 63
- 9.7 Parasol in action — 64
- 9.8 Testing the page title — 65

9.9	Testing displayed information	66
9.10	Testing interactions	68
9.11	Conclusion	73

10 MockObject and Teachable: Two simple mocking approaches   75

10.1	About MockObject design	75
10.2	MockObject	76
10.3	Stubs, Fakes, and Mocks	77
10.4	Example	77
10.5	About matching arguments	78
10.6	Teachable	79
10.7	Conclusion	80

11 Performance testing with SMark   81

11.1	Installing SMark	81
11.2	Measuring execution time	82
11.3	A first benchmark in SMark	83
11.4	Setup and teardown	83
11.5	SMark benchmark runners	84
11.6	Benchmark suites	85
11.7	Result reports	85
11.8	Conclusion	86

CHAPTER 1

Introduction

Pharo is a unique environment in which you can write a test, execute it, and from the raised debugger grow your program. We coined this powerful technique Xtreme Test-Driven Design. This is powerful because it gives you a unique situation where you are in close contact with the specific state of your program. There you can write your code interacting with a live organism (the set of objects that are currently executing your program). It gives you a unique opportunity to query and interact deeply with your objects. Another important point is that tests are at the center of your development flow, not just because you were told to do so but because tests help you develop faster and more robust software.

Describing Xtreme Test-Driven Development feels like describing swimming among the fishes in a scuba diving session. It is difficult to transmit the sensation. Still, we explain Xtreme TDD in a full chapter using a simple example. Since Xtreme Test-Driven Development takes its root in unit testing, we will describe unit testing in Pharo.

1.1 Outline

In this book, we will present how to test and develop testing strategies in Pharo. We will present the SUnit framework and its extensions. We show that contrary to what is commonly believed, testing UI is possible and that you can take advantage of it. We present how to connect your GitHub repository to take advantage of integration services. We also present how to test web applications. We also show some mocking approaches and show that benchmarks can be also supported even if they are not tests per se. We also describe the framework and its implementation.

1.2 About SUnit

Testing is getting more and more exposure. What is interesting to see is that Pharo inherits SUnit from its ancestors (Smalltalk) and it is worth knowing that most of the Unit frameworks are inheriting from the Smalltalk original version developed by K. Beck.

SUnit is a minimal yet powerful framework that supports the creation and deployment of tests. As might be guessed from its name, the design of SUnit focuses on *Unit Tests*, but in fact, it can be used for integration tests and functional tests as well. SUnit was originally developed by Kent Beck and subsequently extended by Joseph Pelrine and others to incorporate the notion of a resource. Note that the version documented in this chapter and used in Pharo is a modified version of SUnit3.3.

1.3 About typographic conventions

In this book, we use the following conventions. We use the new fluid class syntax introduced in Pharo 9. Fluid means that we use a cascade to define the class elements and omit the empty ones.

When you were used to defining a class as follows:

```
TestCase subclass: #MyExampleSetTest
    instanceVariableNames: 'x y'
    classVariableNames: ''
    package: 'MySetTest'
```

We use the following fluid definition

```
TestCase << #MyExampleSetTest
    slots: { #x . #y };
    package: 'MySetTest'
```

Another point is that we always prefix the method source code with the class of the method. The book shows it as:

```
MyExampleSetTest >> testIncludes
    | full empty |
    full := Set with: 5 with: 6.
    empty := Set new.
    self assert: (full includes: 5).
    self assert: (full includes: 6).
    self assert: (empty includes: 5) not
```

And it you want to type it into Pharo you should type the following in the corresponding class.

```
testIncludes
    | full empty |
    full := Set with: 5 with: 6.
    empty := Set new.
    self assert: (full includes: 5).
    self assert: (full includes: 6).
    self assert: (empty includes: 5) not
```

1.4 About this book

In Pharo by Example current revision (9), we decided to go to the essential of SUnit and removed parts that were too detailed and long. This gave us the idea that a "Testing in Pharo" book was missing. Therefore instead of losing the parts that we removed, they grew in a new book. Therefore a part of the text of this book was written originally in Pharo by Example by Andrew P. Black, Stéphane Ducasse, Oscar Nierstrasz, Damien Pollet, Damien Cassou, and Marcus Denker, it is mainly the motivation, description of SUnit and SUnit implementation. We thank them for this material that we revised. Our ultimate goal is to revisit the implementation of SUnit and to keep this book up to date.

Acknowledgments.

We want to thank Jimmie Houchin for improving the English of this book.

1.5 Getting started

We encourage you to experience Test-Driven Development and in particular Xtreme Test-Driven Development. Yes, writing tests looks like an extra effort but it is really worth it. Tests force you to design APIs. They give you insurance so that you will be able to change your code without fear to break your code and not getting notified about it.

CHAPTER 2

Two minutes of theory

The interest in testing and Test Driven Development is not limited to Pharo. Automated testing has become a hallmark of the *Agile software development* movement, and any software developer concerned with improving software quality would do well to adopt it. Indeed, developers in many languages have come to appreciate the power of unit testing. And versions of *xUnit* now exist for every programming language.

What you will discover while programming in Pharo is that Pharo supports *Xtreme TDD*: you define your tests first as in TDD but you execute your program which breaks and then you code in the debugger. This is simply such a productivity boost that we urge you to try it. We are just addicted to it. In Pharo this is super cool to define a test, run the code, and code in the debugger: this is such a speed-up and positive energy.

Now lets us go for two minutes of theory around Unit tests and TDD.

2.1 Automated tests

Neither testing nor the building of test suites is new. By now, everybody knows that tests are a good way to catch errors. eXtreme Programming, by making testing a core practice and by emphasizing *automated* tests, has helped to make testing productive and fun, rather than a chore that programmers dislike. The Pharo community has a long tradition of testing because of the incremental style of development supported by its programming environment.

Favor executable tests

During incremental development sessions in Pharo, the old-fashioned programmer would write code snippets in a playground as soon as a method was finished. Sometimes a test would be incorporated as a comment at the head of the method that it exercised, or tests that needed some setup would be included as example methods in the class. The problem with these practices is that tests in a playground are not available to other programmers who modify the code. Comments and example methods are better in this respect, but there is still no easy way to keep track of them and to run them automatically. Tests that are not **systematically** run do not help you to find bugs! Moreover, an example method does not inform the reader of the expected result: you can run the example and see the (perhaps surprising) result, but you will not know if the observed behavior is correct.

Favor TDD and XtremeTDD

With Test-driven development, you write a little automated test and execute it to make sure that it fails. Then in Pharo, you use the test execution and failure to create methods inside the debugger. Once your test passes, you rerun all your tests and commit if they are all passing.

SUnit is valuable to support this scenario. It allows us to write tests that are automated and self-checking: the test itself defines what the correct result should be. It also helps us to organize tests into groups, describe the context in which the tests must run, and run a group of tests automatically. In less than two minutes you can write tests using SUnit, so instead of writing small code snippets in a playground, we encourage you to use SUnit and get all the advantages of stored and automatically executable tests.

2.2 Why testing is important

Unfortunately, many developers believe that tests are a waste of their time. After all, *they* do not write bugs, only *other* programmers do that. Most of us have said, at some time or other: *I would write tests if I had more time.* If you never write a bug, and if your code will never be changed in the future, then indeed tests are a waste of your time. However, this most likely also means that your application is trivial, or that it is not used by you or anyone else. Think of tests as an investment for the future: having a suite of tests is quite useful now, but it will be *extremely* useful when your application, or the environment in which it runs, changes in the future.

Tests play several roles. First, they provide documentation of the functionality that they cover. This documentation is active: watching the tests pass tells you that the documentation is up to date. Second, tests help developers to confirm that some changes that they have just made to a package have not broken anything else in the system, and to find the parts that break when that confidence turns out to be misplaced. Finally, writing tests during, or even before, programming forces you to think about the functionality that you want to design, *and how it should appear to the client code*, rather than about how to implement it.

By writing the tests first, i.e., before the code, you are compelled to state the context in which your functionality will run, the way it will interact with the client code, and the expected results. Your code will improve. Try it.

We cannot test all aspects of any realistic application. Covering a complete application is simply impossible and should not be the goal of testing. Even with a good test suite, some bugs will still creep into the application, where they can lay dormant waiting for an opportunity to damage your system. If you find that this has happened, take advantage of it! As soon as you uncover the bug, write a test that exposes it, run the test, and watch it fail. Now you can start to fix the bug: the test will tell you when you are done.

2.3 What makes a good test?

Writing good tests is a skill that can be learned by practicing. Let us look at the properties that tests should have to get the maximum benefit.

Tests should be repeatable. You should be able to run a test as often as you want, and always get the same answer.

Tests should run without human intervention. You should be able to run them unattended.

Tests should tell a story. Each test should cover one aspect of a piece of code. A test should act as a scenario that you or someone else can read to understand a piece of functionality.

Tests should have a change frequency lower than that of the functionality they cover. You do not want to have to change all your tests every time you modify your application. One way to achieve this is to write tests based on the public interfaces of the class that you are testing. It is OK to write a test for a private *helper* method if you feel that the method is complicated enough to need the test, but you should be aware that such a test may have to be changed, or thrown away entirely when you think of a better implementation.

One consequence of such properties is that the number of tests should be somewhat proportional to the number of functions to be tested: changing one aspect of the system should not break all the tests but only a limited number. This is important because having 100 tests fail should send a much stronger message than having 10 tests fail. However, it is not always possible to achieve this ideal: in particular, if a change breaks the initialization of an object or the set-up of a test, it is likely to cause all of the tests to fail.

Several software development methodologies such as *eXtreme Programming* and Test-Driven Development (TDD) advocate writing tests before writing code. This may seem to go against our deep instincts as software developers. All we can say is: go ahead and try it. We have found that writing the tests before the code helps us to know what we want to code, helps us know when we are done, and helps us conceptualize the functionality of a class and to design its interface. Moreover, test-first development gives us the courage to go fast, because we are not afraid that we will forget something important.

Writing tests is not difficult in itself. Choosing *what* to test is much more difficult. Some developers coined the "right-BICEP" principle. It stands for:

- Right: Are the results right?
- B: Are all the boundary conditions correct?
- I: Can you check inverse relationships?
- C: Can you cross-check results using other means?
- E: Can you force error conditions to happen?
- P: Are performance characteristics within bounds?

2.4 A piece of advice on testing

While the mechanics of testing are easy, writing good tests is not. Here is some advice on how to design tests.

Self-contained tests

You do not want to have to change your tests each time you change your code, so try to write the tests so that they are self-contained. This can be difficult but pays off in the long term. Writing tests against stable interfaces supports this effort.

Do not over-test

Try to build your tests so that they do not overlap. It is annoying to have many tests covering the same functionality because one bug in the code will then break many tests at the same time. This is covered by Black's rule, below.

Feathers' rules for unit tests

Michael Feathers, an agile process consultant, and author, writes:

A test is not a unit test if: it talks to the database, it communicates across the network, it touches the file system, it can't run at the same time as any of your other unit tests, or you have to do special things to your environment (such as editing config files) to run it. Tests that do these things aren't bad. Often they are worth writing, and they can be written in a unit test harness. However, it is important to be able to separate them from true unit tests so that we can keep a set of tests that we can run fast whenever we make our changes. Never get yourself into a situation where you don't want to run your unit test suite because it takes too long.

Unit tests vs. Acceptance tests

Unit tests capture one piece of functionality, and as such make it easier to identify bugs in that functionality. As far as possible try to have unit tests for each method that could possibly fail, and group them per class. However, for certain deeply recursive or complex setup situations, it is easier to write tests that represent a scenario in the larger application. These are called acceptance tests (or integration tests, or functional tests).

Tests that break Feathers' rules may make good acceptance tests. Group acceptance tests according to the functionality that they test. For example, if you are writing a compiler, you might write acceptance tests that make assertions about the code generated for each possible source language statement. Such tests might exercise many classes and might take a long time to run because they touch the file system. You can write them using SUnit, but you won't want to run them each time you make a small change, so they should be separated from the true unit tests.

Black's rule of testing

For every test in the system, you should be able to identify some property for which the test increases your confidence. It's obvious that there should be no important property that you are not testing. This rule states the less obvious fact that there should be no test that does not add value to the system by increasing your confidence that a useful property holds. For example, several tests of the same property do no good. In fact, they harm in two ways. First, they make it harder to infer the behavior of the class by reading the tests. Second, because one bug in the code might then break many tests, they make it harder to estimate how many bugs remain in the code. So, have a property in mind when you write a test.

2.5 Pharo testing rules as a conclusion

We can argue over and over why tests are important. The only real way to understand for real their values is by experience.

The Pharo core development has three basic rules for testing. Here they are:

Important: A test that is not automated is not a test.

Important: Everything that is not tested does not exist.

Important: Everything that is not tested will break.

With this in mind, we urge ourselves to write tests. Sometimes we are sloppy and lazy but most of the time we push ourselves to stay bold. We encourage you to do the same.

CHAPTER 3

SUnit by example

In this chapter we present a small example showing how simple it is to use SUnit. Before going into the details of SUnit (see next Chapter), we will show a step-by-step example. We use an example that tests the class Set. Try entering the code as we go along. We will create a test i.e., create a context (also called a fixture), execute a stimulus, and verify that some assertions are working.

If you already read the SUnit chapter on Pharo by Example book you can skip this chapter since the contents are the same.

3.1 Step 1: Create the test class

First, you should create a new subclass of TestCase called MyExampleSetTest that looks like this:

The class MyExampleSetTest groups all the tests related to the class Set. As we will show later, we will use it to define the context in which the tests will run.

The name of the class is not critical, but by convention, it should end in Test. If you define a class called Pattern and call the corresponding test class PatternTest, the two classes will be alphabetized together in the browser (as-

Listing 3-1 An Example Set Test class
```
TestCase << #MyExampleSetTest
  package: 'MySetTest'
```

Listing 3-2 Testing includes
```
MyExampleSetTest >> testIncludes
    | full empty |
    full := Set with: 5 with: 6.
    empty := Set new.
    self assert: (full includes: 5).
    self assert: (full includes: 6).
    self assert: (empty includes: 5) not
```

suming that they are in the same package). It *is critical* that your class is a subclass of `TestCase`.

Must I subclass TestCase?

In JUnit you can build a TestSuite from an arbitrary class containing `test*` methods. In SUnit you can do the same but you will then have to create a suite by hand and your class will have to implement all the essential `TestCase` methods like `assert:`. We recommend, however, that you not try to do this. The framework is there: use it.

3.2 Step 2: A first test

We start by defining a method named `testIncludes`. Pay attention to the `'test'` part is important. Each method represents one test. The names of the methods should start with the string `'test'` so that SUnit will collect them into test suites. Test methods take no arguments.

This method creates two sets one empty and one full. This is the context or fixture of the test. Second we perform some action on the test: here we execute the method `includes:`, and third we validate the output using assertion via the `assert:` message. The method `assert:` checks that the argument is a boolean true.

Define the following test methods. The first test, named `testIncludes`, tests the `includes:` method of `Set`. For example, the test says that sending the message `includes:` 5 to a set containing 5 should return `true`.

3.3 Step 3: Run the tests

The easiest way to run the tests is directly from the browser. Press on the icon on the side of the class name, or on an individual test method. The test methods will be flagged depending on whether they pass or not (as shown in 3-3).

3.4 Step 4: Another test

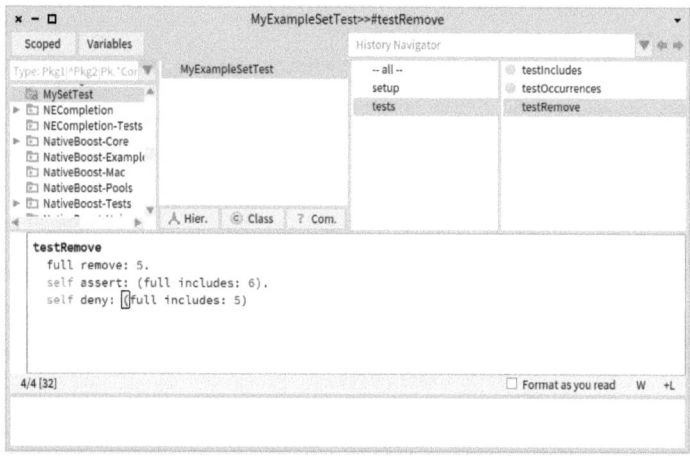

Figure 3-3 Running SUnit tests from the System Browser.

Listing 3-4   Testing occurrences
```
MyExampleSetTest >> testOccurrences
    | full empty |
    full := Set with: 5 with: 6.
    empty := Set new.
    self assert: (empty occurrencesOf: 0) equals: 0.
    self assert: (full occurrencesOf: 5) equals: 1.
    full add: 5.
    self assert: (full occurrencesOf: 5) equals: 1
```

3.4 Step 4: Another test

Following the same pattern, here is a test verifying that the method `occurrencesOf:` works as expected. The second test, named `testOccurrences`, verifies that the number of occurrences of 5 in `full` set is equal to one, even if we add another element 5 to the set.

Note that we use the message `assert:equals:` and not `assert:` as in the first test. We could have used `assert:`. But the message `assert:equals:` is better since it reports the error in a much better way. When an assertion is failing, `assert:equals:` shows the expected value and the value received. While `assert:` just mentions that something is not true.

Now make sure that your test is passing too.

Listing 3-5 An Example Set Test class

```
TestCase << #MyExampleSetTest
    slots: { #full . #empty};
    package: 'MySetTest'
```

Listing 3-6 Setting up a fixture

```
MyExampleSetTest >> setUp
    super setUp.
    empty := Set new.
    full := Set with: 5 with: 6
```

3.5 Step 5: Factoring out context

As you see in the two previous steps, we started to repeat the same context. This is not really nice, so we will factor the fixture out of the tests by defining instance variables in the class and a method setUp to initialize them.

A TestCase class defines the context in which the tests will run. We will add the two instance variables full and empty that we will use to represent a full and an empty set.

The next step is to initialize such instance variables.

3.6 Step 6: Initialize the test context

The message TestCase >> setUp defines the context in which the tests will run, a bit like an initialize method. setUp is invoked before the execution of each test method defined in the test class.

Define the setUp method as follows, to initialize the empty variable to refer to an empty set and the full variable to refer to a set containing two elements.

In testing jargon, the context is called the *fixture* for the test and the setUp method is responsible to initialize such fixture.

Updating existing tests

We change the two test methods to take advantage of the shared initialization. We remove the fixture code and obtain the following methods:

Clearly, these tests rely on the fact that the setUp method has already run.

Taking advantage of setUp

We test that the set no longer contains the element 5 after we have removed it.

3.7 Step 7: Debugging a test

Listing 3-7 Testing includes

```
MyExampleSetTest >> testIncludes

  self assert: (full includes: 5).
  self assert: (full includes: 6).
  self assert: (empty includes: 5) not
```

Listing 3-8 Testing occurrences

```
MyExampleSetTest >> testOccurrences

  self assert: (empty occurrencesOf: 0) equals: 0.
  self assert: (full occurrencesOf: 5) equals: 1.
  full add: 5.
  self assert: (full occurrencesOf: 5) equals: 1
```

Listing 3-9 Testing removal

```
MyExampleSetTest >> testRemove
  full remove: 5.
  self assert: (full includes: 6).
  self deny: (full includes: 5)
```

Note the use of the method `TestCase >> deny:` to assert something that should not be true. `aTest deny: anExpression` is equivalent to `aTest assert: anExpression not`, but is much more readable and expresses the intent more clearly.

3.7 Step 7: Debugging a test

Introduce a bug in `MyExampleSetTest >> testRemove` and run the tests again. For example, change 6 to 7, as in:

The tests that did not pass (if any) are listed in the right-hand panes of the *Test Runner*. If you want to debug one, to see why it failed, just click on the name. Alternatively, you can execute one of the following expressions:

```
(MyExampleSetTest selector: #testRemove) debug

MyExampleSetTest debug: #testRemove
```

Listing 3-10 Introducing a bug in a test

```
MyExampleSetTest >> testRemove
  full remove: 5.
  self assert: (full includes: 7).
  self deny: (full includes: 5)
```

15

3.8 Step 8: Interpret the results

The method `assert:` is defined in the class `TestAsserter`. This is a superclass of `TestCase` and therefore all other `TestCase` subclasses and is responsible for all kinds of test result assertions. The `assert:` method expects a boolean argument, usually the value of a tested expression. When the argument is true, the test passes; when the argument is false, the test fails.

There are actually three possible outcomes of a test: *passing*, *failing*, and *raising an error*.

- **Passing**. The outcome that we hope for is that all of the assertions in the test are true, in which case the test passes. In the test runner, when all of the tests pass, the bar at the top turns green. However, there are two other ways that running a test can go wrong.

- **Failing**. The obvious way is that one of the assertions can be false, causing the test to *fail*.

- **Error**. The other possibility is that some kind of error occurs during the execution of the test, such as a *message not understood* error or an *index out of bounds* error. If an error occurs, the assertions in the test method may not have been executed at all, so we can't say that the test has failed; nevertheless, something is clearly wrong!

In the *test runner*, failing tests cause the bar at the top to turn yellow, and are listed in the middle pane on the right, whereas tests with errors cause the bar to turn red, and are listed in the bottom pane on the right.

Modify your tests to provoke both errors and failures.

3.9 Conclusion

- To maximize their potential, unit tests should be fast, repeatable, independent of any direct human interaction, and cover a single unit of functionality.
- Tests for a class called `MyClass` belong in a class named `MyClassTest`, which should be introduced as a subclass of `TestCase`.
- Initialize your test data in a `setUp` method.
- Each test method should start with the word *test*.
- Use the `TestCase` methods `assert:`, `deny:` and others to make assertions.
- Run tests!

CHAPTER 4

Extreme Test-Driven Development by Example

In this chapter we will describe eXtreme Test-Driven Development (XTDD). XTDD is a unique feature of Pharo and its tools. We show that XTDD is Test-Driven Development on steroids. What is really exciting is that XTDD takes live programming at its best. It shows that in Pharo we can develop smart tools that offer to developers an absolutely gorgeous development flow.

4.1 A simple and powerful principle

The main idea behind XTDD is to avoid breaking the development flow and to take advantage of live programming. It is as simple as:

- First, you write a test.
- Second, you execute the test.
- When it breaks, you define classes, methods, or add instance variables on the fly in the debugger.
- Then, you resume the execution from the debugger and continue the execution until the test is green.

What you should see is that there is no border between specifying a test and developing the code under test. You develop in the flow of the executed program interacting with the objects as you go along.

4.2 Studying an example

Let us illustrate eXtreme Test-Driven Development. We use a dead simple counter. Nothing simpler. This way we will focus on the essence of the process. We want to show you that you can do it.

Basically we will define a test, and the system will help define missing entities (classes). Then we will execute the test. It will break and via the debugger, we will create new methods, add new instance variables and continue the execution without getting out of the debugger.

Let us get started.

4.3 Before executing a test

Define a package and an empty test case class

First we define a package Counter and define a subclass of TestCase named CounterTest.

```
TestCase << #CounterTest
    package: 'Counter'
```

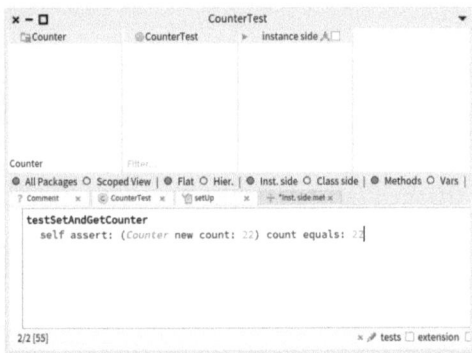

Figure 4-1 Pharo class browser shows the class Counter slanted because that class does not exist.

Define a first test

We define a first test testSetAndGetCounter that

- creates a new instance of the class Counter,
- defines its count value using the setter count:,

4.4 Executing a test to define missing methods

- and verifies that the count value is correct.

```
CounterTest >> testSetAndGetCounter
    self assert: (Counter new count: 22) count equals: 22
```

Now during the definition of the method, the system will notify you because the class Counter does not exist. Figure 4-1 shows that the IDE presents the class Counter slanted to show that this class does not exist.

When you compile the method, the system asks you to define the missing class (see Figure 4-2).

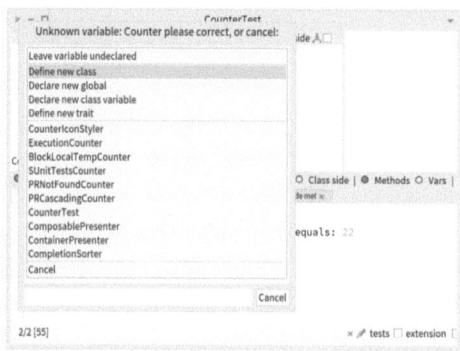

Figure 4-2 Pharo class browser request actions to handle the fact that the class Counter is undefined.

Finally, the class browser proposes you a class definition so that you can define the missing class on the spot (See Figure 4-3). Once the class is defined you will see that it is not slanted anymore in the class browser. And you are ready to execute the test even if you did not define any method yet! This is the whole point of XTDD.

4.4 Executing a test to define missing methods

Even if we did not define any methods yet, we will execute the test. We will just press the little grey button on the left of the method name in the rightmost list as shown in Figure 4-4. It will raise an error because the methods count: and count are not defined.

Figure 4-5 shows the debugger. It indicates that an instance of the class Counter did not understand the message count:. So far so good, this is what we expected.

Extreme Test-Driven Development by Example

Figure 4-3 Pharo class browser proposes a class definition for the class Counter.

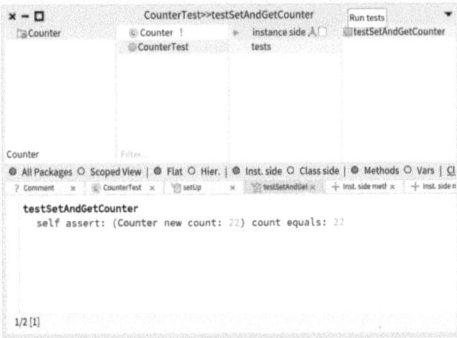

Figure 4-4 Executing a test pressing the grey button on the left of the method name will raise an error.

Define a method on the fly

Now we are ready to create a method on the fly. Just press the button Create. You will get prompted for the class: pick up the class Counter.

The debugger will show you that the system created a generic method named count: for you. It is generic because there is no magic. As shown in Figure 4-6, this method is the following one:

```
Counter >> count: anInteger
    self shouldBeImplemented
```

The message shouldBeImplemented is just a method to raise a specific error. So that the debugger reopens and you can redefine the method.

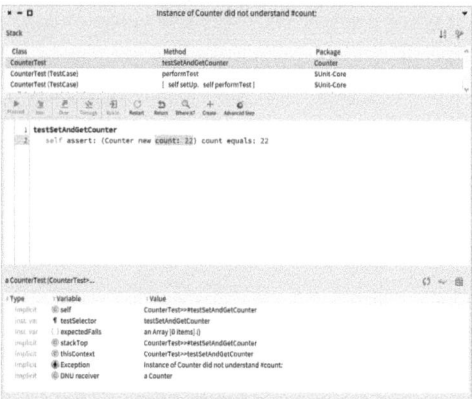

Figure 4-5 A debugger showing that the method count: is not defined hence led to an error.

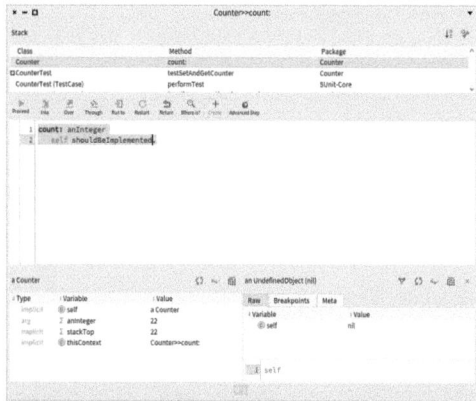

Figure 4-6 The system defined a generic method and restarted the execution: it is now waiting for a definition.

Edit the method in the debugger

Now just edit the method right in the debugger as follows and shown in Figure 4-7. Here we just want a setter that sets the value of the instance variable count. So we just type it!

```
count: anInteger
    count := anInteger
```

Here we define the method as we want it and yes the instance variable count does not exist yet. Do it and compile the method. The class browser will prompt you for the creation of count as an instance variable.

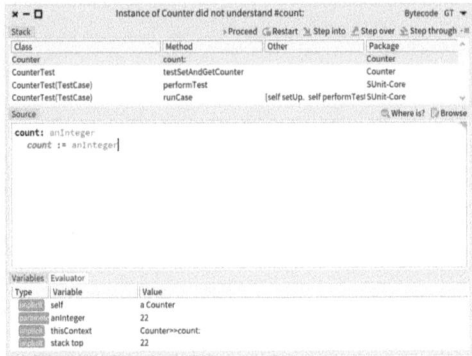

Figure 4-7 Before compiling the method, the class browser shows us that the instance variable count does not exist yet.

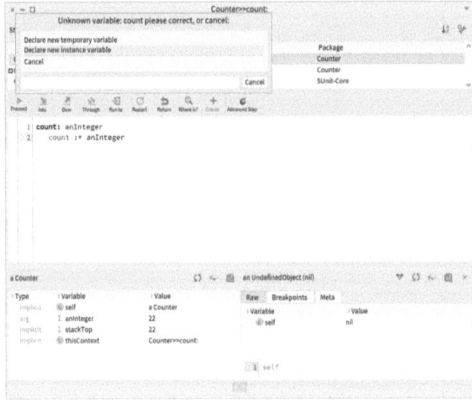

Figure 4-8 Defining a new instance variable from within the debugger.

4.5 Stepping back: Supporting the programmer flow

Compile the method, answer the prompt and you should get the method that we defined previously. Now continue the execution by pressing the Proceed button.

The system will fail again because we did not define the method count as shown in Figure 4-9. You should just add this method as previously shown.

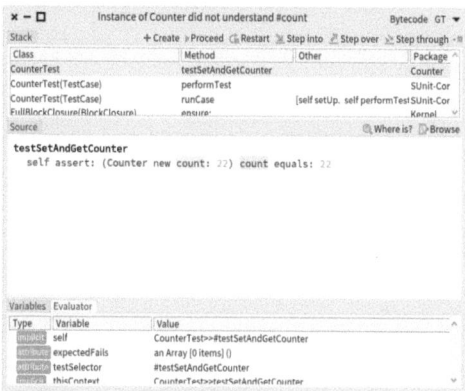

Figure 4-9 The debugger opens because the method count was not defined.

Now notice that the compiler is guessing that the method is an accessor since it has the same name as the instance variable count (see Figure 4-10). It proposes you the method body as:

```
Counter >> count
    ^ count
```

So just accept and press proceed. Your test should be green and you get done.

4.5 Stepping back: Supporting the programmer flow

The system performed several actions to improve the flow of programming:

- It created new methods for us.
- It removed from the stack, the element with Error.
- It replaced it by re-executing the method that was invoking the missing one.
- It relaunched the execution so that we can define the method and proceed with the execution.

We edited and recompiled the method. And we could continue within the exact same flow of programming.

Figure 4-10 Compiler proposed a definition for your accessor.

4.6 One cycle

We show you one simple cycle and now you are ready to:

- Run all the tests to check if nothing was broken.
- Commit your changes if the tests are green.
- Write a new test for the next cycle.

4.7 Why XTDD is powerful?

EXtreme Test-Driven development is powerful because for the following reasons:

- You do not have to guess what will be the exact context of the call of a method. Since you are in the debugger you can access all the objects (receiver or arguments), and you can inspect their specific state. So you avoid guessing, the objects are at your fingers just interact with them to validate the hypotheses you need for defining your methods.
- Tests are not a side effect artifact but a strong driving force.
- The development flow is smooth and strongly connected with your scenario. You write a test and use the test execution to define a context

that helps you define the method. You define methods or instance variables as you go and when you need them. You do not have to plan and guess in advance.

4.7 Why XTDD is powerful?

Protip from expert Pharo developers

Pharo pro developers know what they can gain from XTDD this is why they try to grab an instance as fast as they can and send this object a message. The best way is to write a test fixture and execute it.

CHAPTER 5

SUnit: The framework

Now that you see that writing a test is easy, we will take the time to put into perspective the different aspects of SUnit. SUnit is a framework in the sense that it proposes an architecture that can be adapted. We will not cover the techniques to extend the framework but we will present the key classes and discuss some important points.

5.1 Understanding the framework

What we saw in the previous chapter is that a test method defines a test. Now there is a catch:

- A method (called a test method) of a subclass of the class TestCase represents a test.
- A TestCase subclass groups together all the tests sharing a similar context, called a *fixture*.
- A setUp method is run systematically before a test method is run and a tearDown after.
- The framework builds a TestSuite (a composite of tests) to execute the tests.

5.2 During test execution

Figure 5-1 shows the steps during the execution run of a test:

- An instance of TestCase is created.

- It creates an instance of `TestResult`.
- This instance calls back the `TestCase` instance which executes
    - the test `setUp`
    - the test method
    - and finally the test `tearDown` method.

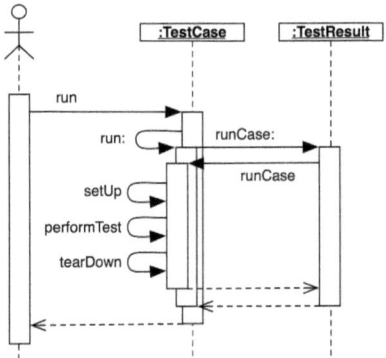

Figure 5-1 During `run` execution.

In fact, the framework ensures that any test method is always surrounded by the execution of the `setUp` and `tearDown` methods. Figure 5-2 illustrates this point. It ensures that the fixture is always in a correct state and avoids dependencies between test execution.

Figure 5-2 `setUp` and `tearDown` in action.

5.3 The framework in a nutshell

SUnit consists of four main classes: `TestCase`, `TestSuite`, `TestResult`, and `TestResource`, as shown in Figure 5-3.

5.3 The framework in a nutshell

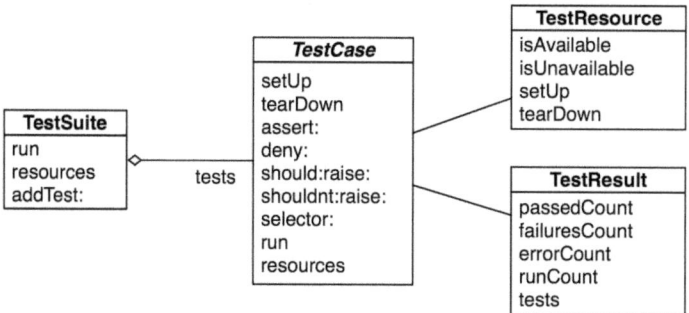

Figure 5-3 The four classes representing the core of SUnit.

TestCase

TestCase is an abstract class that is designed to be subclassed. Each of its subclasses represents a **group** of tests that share a common context: such a group is called a **test suite**.

Each test is run by creating a new instance of a subclass of TestCase, running setUp to initialize the test fixture, running the test method itself, and then sending the tearDown to clean up the test fixture.

The fixture is specified by instance variables of the subclass and by the specialization of the method setUp, which initializes those instance variables. Subclasses of TestCase can also override method tearDown, which is invoked after the execution of each test, and can be used to release any objects allocated during setUp.

TestSuite

Instances of the class TestSuite contain a collection of test cases. An instance of TestSuite contains tests and other test suites. That is, a test suite contains sub-instances of TestCase and TestSuite. Both individual test cases and test suites understand the same protocol, so they can be treated in the same way (for example, both can be run). This is in fact an application of the Composite pattern in which TestSuite is the composite and the test cases are the leaves.

TestResult

The class TestResult represents the results of a TestSuite execution. It records the number of tests passed, the number of tests failed, and the number of errors signaled.

Listing 5-4 Testing removal of a non-existing element.
```
MyExampleSetTest >> testRemoveNonexistentElement
  empty remove: 5.
```

Listing 5-5 Testing removal of a non-existing element.
```
MyExampleSetTest >> testRemoveNonexistentElement

  self should: [ empty remove: 5 ] raise: NotFound
```

TestResources

The notion of a *test resource* represents a resource that is expensive to set-up but which can be used by a whole series of tests. A `TestResource` specifies a `setUp` method that is executed just once before a full suite of tests; this is in distinction to the `TestCase >> setUp` method, which is executed before each test. The class `TestResource` represents resources that can be shared among a test suite: Subclasses of `TestResource` are associated with test case classes and this means that all the suite of tests represented by the test case class (See Chapter 6).

5.4 Test states

As we mentioned earlier, the result of a test execution is mainly: passed (meaning that it succeeded), fails (that an assertion is not valid) or error (that an unexpected problem occurred).

Failures vs. Error

In fact, this is really important to understand the difference between a failure and an error. A failure is something that you plan and you check whether is happened or not. When it happens your tests pass, or else it fails.

Removing an element that is not in a set from that set raises an error. If we write the following test, the test will fail.

Now using the message `should:raise:` we make sure that we check that the expression effectively raises an error. It means that our test can either pass (i.e., it means that the test fulfills our requirement here that it should raise an error when removing an unknown element) or fail. We planned such behavior. It can fail or pass.

For an error this is different, an error occurs in an unplanned manner. The execution of the first version of `testRemoveNonexistentElement` would lead to an error.

5.5 Glossary

Listing 5-6 An example of a skipped test.
```
MyExampleSetTest >> testToBeRevisitedLater

  self skip.
  ...
```

Listing 5-7 A not so nice example of a skipped test.
```
MyExampleSetTest >> testToBeRevisitedLater

  true ifTrue: [^ self ].
  ...
```

Expected Failures and Skip

In addition, a test can be in two other states: skipped and expected failures. Such states are handy during development.

The idea is that if you write a complex test and suddenly you realize that you will have more work than expected to make your test pass, you can mark it as skipped.

In fact, it is much better to use the message `skip` than to use a guard. Why because the framework can report clearly that your test is skipped. Using a guard as below is the best way to confuse yourself because the framework will return that the test passes while it does NOT.

You can also tag your test with the `<expectedFailure>` pragma to indicate to the framework that you expect your test to fail. This is to be taken into account by the framework when running and reporting all your tests. Hence you will be aware that some of your tests did not run correctly. Here is an example from Pharo.

```
testFromClassWhichTraitIsExtendedButNotItself
  "I'm tagging this expected failure because I'm not sure now if it is
    appropriate to keep
  or not with the removal of the 'traits-as-multiple-inheritance'
    stuff."
  <expectedFailure>

  self queryFromScope: ClyClassScope of: ClyClassWithTraits.
  self assert: resultItems size equals: 0
```

5.5 Glossary

- **Test case.** A test case is a single test. It defines a context, a stimulus, and at the minimum one assertion. It is described as a method of a TestCase subclass starting with **test**.

- **Test suite.** A test suite (Composite design pattern) is a group of tests. The tests belonging to a test suite do not have to be from the same class. In practice, the test runner builds a test suite for all the test cases defined in a class and executes them one by one. Instances of the class TestSuite contain a collection of test cases. An instance of TestSuite contains tests and other test suites. That is, a test suite contains sub-instances of TestCase and TestSuite.

- **Fixture.** A fixture is a context in which a stimulus will be executed and assertions verified. To share a fixture amongst multiple tests you can define the setUp method. It is automatically invoked before any test method execution.

- **Failure.** A failure is the situation where you planned something and checked it and it is not correct.

- **Error.** An error is the situation where your test is not working but it is not covered by an assertion. For example, a message not understood is sent and it was unexpected.

5.6 Chapter summary

In this chapter we gave an overview of the core of the SUnit framework by presenting the classes TestCase, TestResult, TestSuite andTestResources. We described the setUp/tearDown logic and the different states a test can be in.

CHAPTER 6

A little cookbook

This chapter will give you more details on the possibilities offered to you to express tests. We will start to show that we can also have method comments that are automatically validated and that such executable comments are similar to elementary unit tests.

Note that if you have used another testing framework such as JUnit, much of this will be familiar, since all these frameworks have their roots in SUnit. We will also present a powerful feature of SUnit: parametrized tests.

6.1 Testing comments

Often you would like to comment your methods with little examples. The problem with putting code snippets in the comment of a method is that they are doomed to rot. And you do not have an easy way to find outdated comments.

This is why, in Pharo, you can also use executable comments to document your methods. An executable comment is a comment containing Pharo code but that follows a certain form (expression >>> resulting expression). This form makes sure that the IDE can check if they are still valid.

Let us look at an example from the class ==String==.

```
String >> asCamelCase
    "Convert to CamelCase, i.e, remove spaces, and convert starting
    lowercase to uppercase."

    "'A man, a plan, a canal, panama' asCamelCase >>>
```

```
    'AMan,APlan,ACanal,Panama'"
"'Here 123should % be 6 the name6 of the method' asCamelCase >>>
    'Here123should%Be6TheName6OfTheMethod'"

^ self species streamContents: [:stream |
        self substrings do: [:sub |
                stream nextPutAll: sub capitalized]]
```

The comment `"'A man, a plan, a canal, panama' asCamelCase >>> 'AMan,APlan,ACanal,Panama'"` is an executable comment. It is delimited by `"` and `>>>`.

- The message `>>>` delimits the expression from its result.
- On the left, we get the expression.
- On the right, we get the result.

This way a tool can verify that the comment is correct.

6.2 Parameterized tests

Since Pharo 7.0 you can express parameterized tests. Parametrized tests are tests that can be executed on multiple configurations: your tests will run on different contexts that you can specify basically as test arguments. Parametrized tests are really powerful when you want to check whether two implementations pass the same set of tests.

To declare a parameterized test you have to:

- define your test case class as a subclass of `ParametrizedTestCase` instead of `TestCase`. This class should define accessors that will be used to configure the tests.
- define a *class* method named `testParameters` which specifies the actual parameters.

A simple example first

Here is an example taken from the Enlumineur project which is a pretty printer for Pharo code. Using parametrized tests lets us know whether two different pretty printers produce the same outputs.

We define the class `BIEnlumineurTest`. It has different parameters expressed as instance variables such as `formatterClass` and `contextClass`.

```
ParametrizedTestCase <<: #BIEnlumineurTest
    slots: { #configurationSelector . #formatterClass . #contextClass};
    package: 'Enlumineur-Tests'
```

This class should define accessors for its parameters, here for `formatterClass` and `contextClass`. The tests should use the test instance variables and should not refer directly to the classes held by the instance variables. Else this would shortcut the idea of a parametrized test itself.

Then we define the class method `testParameters` as follows.

```
BIEnlumineurTest class >> testParameters
  ^ ParametrizedTestMatrix new
    addCase: { (#formatterClass -> BIEnlumineurPrettyPrinter) .
    (#contextClass -> BIEnlumineurContext) };
    yourself
```

Now the framework will run the test using the parameters we mentioned. To add a new variation we just have to add a case using the `addCase:` message.

Controlling configuration

The following example generates 2 cases. Exactly the 2 cases listed in `testParameters` method. The values for `number1` and `number2` will be set and the test will be executed.

```
PaSelectedCasesExampleTest class >> testParameters

  ^ ParametrizedTestMatrix new
    addCase: { #number1 -> 2. #number2 -> 1.0. #result -> 3 };
    addCase: { #number1 -> (2/3). #number2 -> (1/3). #result -> 1 };
    yourself
```

6.3 Matrix: a more advanced case

Sometimes you do not want to enumerate all the combinations by hand. In that case, you can use a matrix and specify all the possible values of a parameter. The class `PaSimpleMatrixExampleTest` contains some examples.

The following test executes 27 different cases. All the combinations in the matrix are executed, i.e. item1 values will be enumerated, and for each one, all the values of the other parameters will be also enumerated. This way all possible combinations are generated and tests run for each of them.

```
PaSimpleMatrixExampleTest class >> testParameters

  ^ ParametrizedTestMatrix new
    forSelector: #item1 addOptions: { 1. 'a'. $c };
    forSelector: #item2 addOptions: { 2. 'b'. $d };
    forSelector: #collectionClass addOptions: { Set. Bag.
    OrderedCollection }
```

The test matrix generates using a cartesian product the configurations or a set of well-known cases. Each option is constituted from a set of possible values and a selector that is the name of the parameter to set in the test case instance. Another example of testParameters is:

```
testParameters

    ^ ParametrizedTestMatrix new
        forSelector: #option1 addOptions: #(a b c);
        forSelector: #option2 addOptions: {[1].[2].[3]};
        yourself.
```

This example will generate 9 different configurations. One per each combination of option1 and option2. Do not forget that the test case should have a setter for each option.

In addition each option can be a literal or a block to generate that value. The block has an optional parameter, the parameter is the test case to configure.

6.4 Classes vs. objects as parameters

There is a subtle but important point about the kind of parameters. Indeed, we may wonder whether it is better to pass a class or an instance as a parameter of a test. Theoretically, there is not much difference between passing a class or an object. However, in practice, there is a difference because when we pass an object, as in the following configuration, the framework does not recreate the object during each test execution. Therefore if your object accumulates information, then such information will be shared among your tests and this is a bad idea.

```
CbkDlittleImporterTest class >> testParameters

    ^ ParametrizedTestMatrix new
        addCase: { #importer -> CBkCollectorDLittleImporter new };
        yourself.
```

The solution is to favor passing classes as follows and to explicitly create objects in the setUp. This way you are sure that your object does not hold its state from the previous execution.

```
CbkDlittleImporterTest class >> testParameters

    ^ ParametrizedTestMatrix new
        addCase: { #importerClass -> CBkCollectorDLittleImporter };
        yourself.

CbkDlittleImporterTest >> setUp
```

6.5 Other assertions

Listing 6-1 Testing error raising
```
MyExampleSetTest >> testIllegal
    self should: [ empty at: 5 ] raise: Error.
    self should: [ empty at: 5 put: #zork ] raise: Error

    super setUp.
    importer := importerClass new.

CbkDlittleImporterTest >> importerClass: anImporterClass
    importerClass := anImporterClass
```

In conclusion, we suggest passing instances as parameters when the objects are not complex and to favor classes otherwise.

6.5 Other assertions

In addition to `assert:` and `deny:`, there are several other methods that can be used to make assertions.

First, `TestAsserter >> assert:description:` and `TestAsserter >> deny:description:` take a second argument which is a message string that describes the reason for the failure, if it is not obvious from the test itself. These methods are described in Section 6.5.

Next, SUnit provides two additional methods, `TestAsserter >> should:raise:` and `TestAsserter >> shouldnt:raise:` for testing exception propagation.

For example, you would use `self should: aBlock raise: anException` to test that a particular exception is raised during the execution of aBlock. The method below illustrates the use of `should:raise:`.

Try running this test. Note that the first argument of the `should:` and `shouldnt:` methods is a block that contains the expression to be executed.

Note that this is usually not good to catch exceptions using the `Error` class since it is catching basically everything. In that current case, the `at:` primitive signals an instance of `Error` so we have to deal with it.

Using `assert:equals:`

In addition to `assert:`, there is also `assert:equals:` that offers a better report in case of error (incidentally, `assert:equals:` uses `assert:description:`).

For example, the two following tests are equivalent. However, the second one will report the value that the test is expecting: this makes it easier to understand the failure. In this example, we suppose that aDateAndTime is an instance variable of the test class.

```
testAsDate
  self assert: aDateAndTime asDate = ('February 29, 2004' asDate
    translateTo: 2 hours).

testAsDate
  self
    assert: aDateAndTime asDate
    equals: ('February 29, 2004' asDate translateTo: 2 hours).
```

Assertion description strings

The TestAsserter assertion protocol includes a number of methods that allow the programmer to supply a description of the assertion. The description is aString; if the test case fails, this string will be displayed by the test runner. Of course, this string can be constructed dynamically.

```
...
e := 42.
self assert: e = 23 description: 'expected 23, got ', e printString
...
```

The relevant methods in TestAsserter are:

```
assert:description:
deny:description:
should:description:
shouldnt:description:
```

6.6 Running tests

Running a single test

Normally, you will run your tests using the Test Runner or using your code browser. You can also run a single test as follows:

```
> MyExampleSetTest run: #testRemove
1 run, 1 passed, 0 failed, 0 errors
```

Running all the tests in a test class

Any subclass of TestCase responds to the message suite, which builds a test suite that contains all the methods in the class whose names start with the string *test*.

To run the tests in the suite, send it the message `run`. For example:

```
> MyExampleSetTest suite run
5 run, 5 passed, 0 failed, 0 errors
```

6.7 Advanced features of SUnit

In addition to `TestResource` that we present just in the subsequent section, SUnit contains assertion description strings, logging support, the ability to skip tests, and resumable test failures.

Logging support

The description strings mentioned above may also be logged to a `Stream`, such as the `Transcript` or a file stream. You can choose whether to log by overriding `isLogging` in your test class; you can also choose where to log by overriding `failureLog` to answer an appropriate stream. By default, the `Transcript` is used to log.

To enable logging, you should redefine the method `isLogging` to say so.

```
MyExampleSetTest class >> isLogging
    ^ true
```

Skipping tests

Sometimes in the middle of a development, you may want to skip a test instead of removing it or renaming it to prevent it from running. You can simply invoke the `TestAsserter` message `skip` on your test case instance. For example, the following test uses it to define a conditional test.

```
OCCompiledMethodIntegrityTest >> testPragmas

    | newCompiledMethod originalCompiledMethod |
    (self class environment hasClassNamed: #Compiler) ifFalse: [ ^ self
        skip ].
    ...
```

It is better to use `skip` than to use a simple `^ self` because in the latter case you may think that your test is executed when it is not!

Continuing after a failure

SUnit also allows us to specify whether or not a test should continue after a failure. This is a really powerful feature that uses Pharo's exception mechanisms. To see what this can be used for, let's look at an example.

Consider the following test expression:

```
[ aCollection do: [ :each | self assert: each even ]
```

In this case, as soon as the test finds the first element of the collection that isn't even, the test stops. However, we would usually like to continue and see both how many elements, and which elements, aren't even (and maybe also log this information).

You can do this as follows:

```
aCollection do: [ :each |
  self
    assert: each even
    description: each printString, ' is not even'
    resumable: true ]
```

This will print out a message on your logging stream for each element that fails. It doesn't accumulate failures, i.e, if the assertion fails 10 times in your test method, you'll still only see one failure. All the other assertion methods that we have seen are not resumable by default;`assert: p description: s` is equivalent to`assert: p description: s resumable: false`.

6.8 Test resources

One of the important features of a suite of tests is that they should be independent of each other. The failure of one test should not cause an avalanche of failures of other tests that depend upon it, nor should the order in which the tests are run matter. Performing `setUp` before each test and `tearDown` afterward helps to reinforce this independence.

However, there are occasions where setting up the necessary context is just too time-consuming for it to be done before the execution of each test. Moreover, if it is known that the test cases do not disrupt the resources used by the tests, then it is wasteful to set them up afresh for each test. It is sufficient to set them up once for each suite of tests. Suppose, for example, that a suite of tests needs to query a database, or do analysis on some compiled code. In such cases, it may make sense to set up the database and open a connection to it, or to compile some source code, before any of the tests start to run.

Where should we cache these resources, so that they can be shared by a suite of tests? The instance variables of a particular `TestCase` subclass won't do, because a TestCase instance persists only for the duration of a single test (as mentioned before, the instance is created anew *for each test method*). A global variable would work, but using too many global variables pollutes the namespace, and the binding between the global and the tests that depend on it will not be explicit.

6.8 Test resources

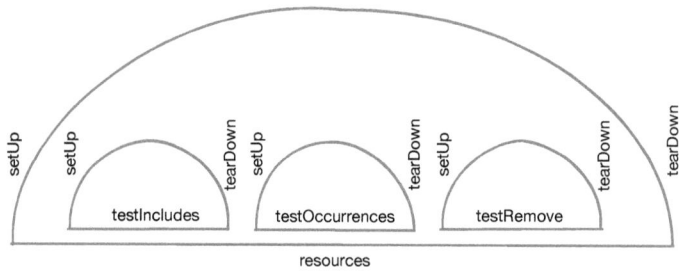

Figure 6-2 setUp and tearDown in action.

Listing 6-3 An example of a TestResource subclass

```
TestResource << #MyTestResource
    package: 'MyPackage'

MyTestResource >> setUp
    ...

MyTestCase class >> resources
    "Associate the resource with this class of test cases"

    ^ { MyTestResource }
```

A better solution is to define a TestResource and use it. The class TestResource implements a singleton to manage the execution of setUp and tearDown around a complete test suite as shown in Figure 6-2. Each subclass of TestResource understands the message current, which will answer a singleton instance of that subclass. Methods setUp and tearDown should be overridden in the subclass to ensure that the resource is initialized and finalized.

One thing remains: somehow, SUnit has to be told which resources are associated with which test suite. A resource is associated with a particular subclass of TestCase by overriding the *class* method resources.

By default, the resources of a TestSuite are the union of the resources of the TestCase's that it contains.

Here is an example. We define a subclass of TestResource called MyTestResource. Then we associate it with MyTestCase by overriding the class method MyTestCase class >> resources to return an array of the test resource classes that MyTestCase will use.

You can also define the instance side method isAvailable to indicate whether the resource is available. But if you need this, better read the code of the TestResource class.

Checking the described behavior

The following trace (written to the `Transcript`) illustrates that a global setup is run before and after each test in a sequence. Let's see if you can obtain this trace yourself.

```
MyTestResource >> setUp has run.
MyTestCase >> setUp has run.
MyTestCase >> testOne has run.
MyTestCase >> tearDown has run.
MyTestCase >> setUp has run.
MyTestCase >> testTwo has run.
MyTestCase >> tearDown has run.
MyTestResource >> tearDown has run.
```

Create new classes `MyTestResource` and `MyTestCase` which are subclasses of`TestResource` and `TestCase` respectively. Add the appropriate methods so that the following messages are written to the `Transcript` when you run your tests.

Solution

You will need to write the following six methods.

```
MyTestCase >> setUp
    Transcript show: 'MyTestCase>>setUp has run.'; cr

MyTestCase >> tearDown
    Transcript show: 'MyTestCase>>tearDown has run.'; cr

MyTestCase >> testOne
    Transcript show: 'MyTestCase>>testOne has run.'; cr

MyTestCase >> testTwo
    Transcript show: 'MyTestCase>>testTwo has run.'; cr

MyTestCase class >> resources
    ^ Array with: MyTestResource

MyTestResource >> setUp
    Transcript show: 'MyTestResource>>setUp has run'; cr

MyTestResource >> tearDown
    Transcript show: 'MyTestResource>>tearDown has run.'; cr
```

6.9 Customising tests: Examples as tests

In this section, we show that SUnit offers two hooks to define what a test selector is and how to perform the test.

Imagine that we want to support example methods as tests. Let us define what are example methods: Let us say that an example method is a class method if its selector follows the pattern example*.

For the sake of simplicity imagine that the method classWithExamplesToTest returns a class defining example methods.

We can then define the method testSelectors as follows:

```
HiExamplesTest class >> testSelectors [
  ^ self classWithExamplesToTest class methods
    select: [ :each | (each selector beginsWith: 'example') and: [
    each numArgs = 0 ] ]
    thenCollect: [ :each | each selector ]
```

Then we can redefine the method performTest to execute the example method on the class itself.

```
HiExamplesTest >> performTest
  example := self class classWithExamplesToTest perform: testSelector
    asSymbol
```

What you can see is that with a couple of methods, we can extend SUnit to support alternative ways to define and execute tests. No need for several tenths of classes as in some solutions.

6.10 Inheriting TestCase

A new TestCase can inherit tests from a superclass. The logic is a bit cumbersome. By default, a new test case class inherits from a subclass of TestCase that is abstract. If your new subclass has no test methods it will inherit from its superclass.

Otherwise, if your new class has selectors and inherits from a concrete superclass, you should redefine shouldInheritSelectors to return true.

What developers use in practice is the last part: to redefine the method shouldInheritSelectors. For example, this is what the CoCompletionEngineTest class is doing to inherit the tests of CompletionEngineTest

```
CoCompletionEngineTest >> shouldInheritSelectors
  ^ true
```

Here is the definition of the method shouldInheritSelectors.

```
TestCase class >> shouldInheritSelectors
    "I should inherit from an Abstract superclass but not from a
      concrete one by default
    unless I have no testSelectors in which case I must be expecting to
      inherit them from my superclass.
    If a test case with selectors wants to inherit selectors from a
      concrete superclass, override this to true in that subclass."

    ^self ~~ self lookupHierarchyRoot
        and: [self superclass isAbstract or: [self testSelectors isEmpty]]
```

6.11 Conclusion

SUnit is a simple framework but it already provides a powerful set of mechanisms to take real advantage of writing tests. In particular parametrized tests are a powerful method when you have several objects that expose the same API, then you can reuse your tests.

CHAPTER 7

SUnit implementation

The implementation of SUnit makes an interesting case study of a Pharo framework. Let's look at some key aspects of the implementation by following the execution of a test.

7.1 Running one test

To execute one test, we execute the expression (aTestClass selector: aSymbol) run.

The method TestCase >> run creates an instance of TestResult that will accumulate the results of the test, then it sends itself the messageTestCase >> run: (See Figure 7-1).

```
TestCase >> run
    | result |
    result := self classForTestResult new.
    [ self run: result ]
        ensure: [ self classForTestResource resetResources: self resources
        ].
    ^ result
```

The method TestCase >> run: sends the message runCase: to the test result:

The method TestResult >> runCase: sends the message TestCase >> runCase to an individual test, to execute the test. TestResult >> runCase deals with any exceptions that may be raised during the execution of a test, runs

SUnit implementation

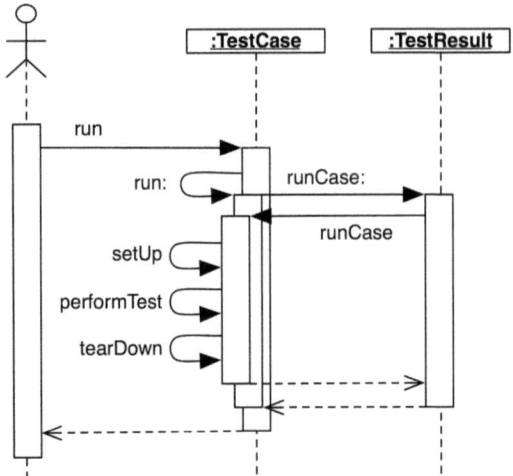

Figure 7-1 Running one test.

Listing 7-2 Passing the test case to the test result
```
TestCase >> run: aResult
    aResult runCase: self
```

Listing 7-3 Catching test case errors and failures
```
TestResult >> runCase: aTestCase
    [
    aTestCase announce: TestCaseStarted withResult: self.
    aTestCase runCase.
    aTestCase announce: TestCaseEnded withResult: self.
    self addPass: aTestCase ]
        on: self class failure, self class skip, self class warning, self
        class error
        do: [ :ex | ex sunitAnnounce: aTestCase toResult: self ]
```

aTestCase by sending it the runCase, and counts the errors, failures, and passes.

The method TestCase >> runCase sends the messages TestCase >> setUp andTestCase >> tearDown as shown below.
```
TestCase >> runCase
    self resources do: [ :each | each availableFor: self ].
    [ self setUp.
    self performTest ] ensure: [
      self tearDown.
```

Listing 7-4   Auto-building the test suite

```
TestCase class >> testSelectors
    ^ (self selectors select: [ :each | (each beginsWith: 'test') and: [
    each numArgs isZero ]])


    self cleanUpInstanceVariables ]
```

7.2   Running a TestSuite

To run more than one test, we send the message run to a TestSuite that contains the relevant tests. TestCase class provides some functionality to build a test suite from its methods. The expression MyTestCase buildSuiteFromSelectors returns a suite containing all the tests defined in the MyTestCase class. The core of this process is:

The method TestSuite >> run creates an instance of TestResult, verifies that all the resources are available, and then sends itself the messageTestSuite >> run:, which runs all the tests in the suite. All the resources are then released.

```
TestSuite >> run: aResult
  self setUp.
  [ self tests
    do: [ :each |
      each run: aResult.
      self announceTest: each.
      self changed: each ] ]
    ensure: [ self tearDown ]

TestSuite >> setUp
  self resources do: [ :each |
        each isAvailable ifFalse: [ each signalInitializationError ]
    ].

TestSuite >> tearDown
    self resourceClass resetResources: self resources
```

The class TestResource and its subclasses keep track of their currently created singleton instances that can be accessed and created using the class method TestResource class >> current. This instance is cleared when the tests have finished running and the resources are reset.

The resource availability check makes it possible for the resource to be re-created if needed, as shown in the class method TestResource class >> isAvailable. During the TestResource instance creation, it is initialized and the message setUp is sent to a test resource.

Listing 7-5 Test resource availability

```
TestResource class >> isAvailable
    "This is (and must be) a lazy method. If my current has a value, an
        attempt to make me available has already been made: trust its
        result. If not, try to make me available."

    current ifNil: [ self makeAvailable ].
    ^ self isAlreadyAvailable
```

Listing 7-6 Test resource creation

```
TestResource class >> current
    "This is a lazy accessor: the assert of self isAvailable does no
        work unless current isNil. However this method should normally be
        sent only to a resource that should already have been made
        available, e.g. in a test whose test case class has the resource
        class in its #resources, so should never be able to fail the
        assert.
    If the intent is indeed to access a possibly-unprepared or
        reset-in-earlier-test resource lazily, then preface the call of
        'MyResource current' with 'MyResource availableFor: self'."

    self
        assert: self isAvailable
        description:
            'Sent #current to unavailable resource ', self name,
               '. Add it to test case'' class-side #resources (recommended)
        or send #availableFor: beforehand'.
    ^ current
```

- To maximize their potential, unit tests should be fast, repeatable, independent of any direct human interaction and cover a single unit of functionality.
- Tests for a class called MyClass belong in a class named MyClassTest, which should be introduced as a subclass of TestCase.
- Initialize your test data in a setUp method.
- Each test method should start with the word *test*.
- Use the TestCase methods assert:, deny: and others to make assertions.
- Run tests!

CHAPTER 8

UI testing

Developers often think that testing UI is difficult. This is true that fully testing the placement and layout of widgets can be tedious. However, testing the logic of an application and in particular the interaction logic is possible and this is what we will show in this chapter. We show that testing Spec application is simple and effective.

8.1 Testing Spec

Tests are key to ensuring that everything works correctly. In addition, they free us from the fear to break something without being warned about it. Tests support refactorings. While such facts are general and applicable to many domains, they are also true for user interfaces.

Spec architecture

Spec is based on an architecture with three different layers as shown in Figure 8-1:

- **Presenters:** Presenters defined the interaction logic and manipulate domain objects. They access back-end widgets but via an API that is specified by Adapters.

- **Adapters:** Adapters are objects exposing low-level back-end widgets. They are a bridge between presenters and low-level widgets.

- **Back-end widgets.** Back-end widgets are plain widgets that can be used without Spec.

49

UI testing

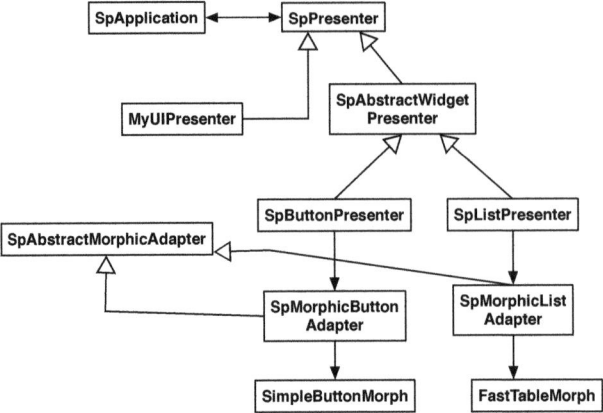

Figure 8-1 Spec Architecture.

Three roles and concerns

To help you understand the different possibilities of testing that you can engage in, we identify the following roles and their related concerns.

- **Spec Users.** Spec users are developers that build a new application. They define the logic of the application by assembling together presenters and domain objects.
- **Spec Developers.** Spec developers are more concerned with the development of new Spec presenters and their links with the adapter.
- **Widget Developers.** Widget developers are concerned about the logic and working of a given widget in a given back-end.

We will focus on the first role. For the reader interested in the second role, the class `SpAbstractBackendForTest` is a good starting place.

8.2 Spec user perspective

As a Spec user, you should consider that the back-ends are working and your responsibility is to test the logic of the user interface components. We should make sure that when the model changes, the user interface components reflect the changes. Inversely when the user interface components change, we should ensure that the model is updated.

8.3 Example

We will test a simple spec application. The model for this application can be any class. It shows in a tree presenter all the subclasses of the model. Also, has a text presenter that shows the definition string for the selected class. Finally, has a string morph and a button. When the button is pressed, the color of the morph changes randomly.

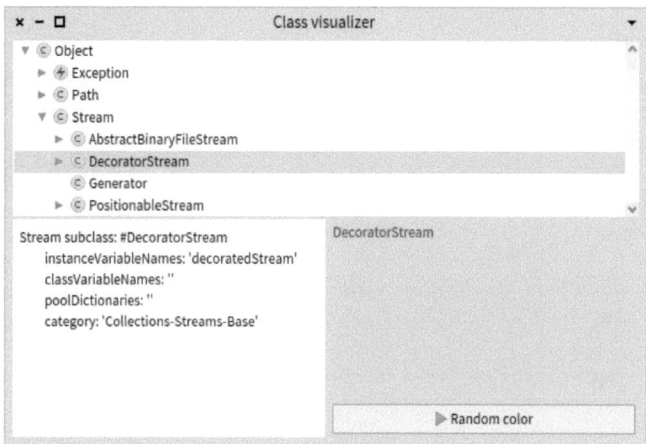

Figure 8-2 A Spec application.

Spec user test 1: correct initialization

The tool will be instantiated with a model. In this case, we will use Object because it is the root of almost all classes. So, when we instantiate the spec application of the figure above, all the sub-presenters of the application must show the data of the model.

```
testInitialization

  | model |
  model := String.
  spApplication := ClassVisualizerPresenter on: model.
  self assert: spApplication model equals: model.
  self
    assert: spApplication textPresenter text
    equals: model classDefinitions first definitionString.
  self
    assert: spApplication morphPresenter morph contents
    equals: model name
```

8.4 Spec user test 2: Tree selection

When selecting a new item in the tree presenter, the text presenter and the morph should change.

The tree presenter shows a tree of classes. When a class of the tree presenter is selected, the text presenter should change according to the definition of the newly selected class. The morph must change as well.

```
testSelectItemOnTreePresenter

  "As we have initialized the tree with Object as its roots. The class
    OrderedCollection is a subclass of Object. We would simulate that
    a user selected OrderedCollection from the tree presenter."

  spApplication := ClassVisualizerPresenter on: Object.
  spApplication hierarchyTreePresenter selectItem: OrderedCollection.
  self
    assert: spApplication hierarchyTreePresenter selectedItem
    equals: OrderedCollection.
  self
    assert: spApplication textPresenter text
    equals: OrderedCollection classDefinitions first definitionString.
  self
    assert: spApplication morphPresenter morph contents
    equals: OrderedCollection name
```

8.5 Spec user test 3: triggering the button action

The action of the color button changes the color of the morph randomly. When the button is clicked the morph must change its color.

```
testButtonChangesMorph

  | previousColor |
  spApplication := ClassVisualizerPresenter on: Object.
  previousColor := spApplication morphPresenter morph color.
  spApplication colorButton click.
  self
    deny: spApplication morphPresenter morph color
    equals: previousColor
```

8.6 Spec user test 4: Not editable text presenter

For this application, we only want that the text presenter shows the class definition. We do not want the user to be able to edit it.

```
testTextPresenterIsNotEditable

    spApplication := ClassVisualizerPresenter on: Object.
    self deny: spApplication textPresenter isEditable
```

8.7 Spec user test 5: the window is built correctly

Here, we will test that the title and the initial extent of the window are correct. Also, we will test if the window was built correctly.

```
testInitializeWindow

    | window |
    spApplication := ClassVisualizerPresenter on: Object.
    window := spApplication openWithSpec.
    self assert: window isBuilt.
    self assert: window title equals: ClassVisualizerPresenter title.
    self assert: window initialExtent equals: 600 @ 400.
    window close
```

8.8 Known limitations and conclusion

We show in this chapter that you can take advantage of Spec to define tests that will help you to evolve the visual part of your application.

Currently, Spec does not offer a way to script and control popup windows. It is not possible to script a button that opens a dialog for a value. Future versions of Spec20 should cover this missing feature.

CHAPTER 9

Testing web applications with Parasol

Chapter Contributors: Evelyn Cusi and Daniel Aparicio

During the construction of a web application, it is exhausting to have to test the entire flow of the application each time you modify it, and much more as the application grows. This chapter introduces Parasol to allow developers to automate tests with a collection of language-specific bindings, giving us the facility to test complex interactions in a matter of seconds.

Parasol, also called *Beach Parasol*, is a Smalltalk framework to write functional/acceptance tests using Selenium WebDriver. Through Parasol, you can access all functionalities of Selenium WebDriver in an intuitive way. Parasol gives a convenient API to access to the WebDrivers of Selenium such as Chrome, Firefox, and others. Actually, Parasol supports recent versions of Pharo and GemStone. Parasol was developed by Johan Brichau and Andy Kellens from Two Rivers.

9.1 Getting started

To load Parasol into your Pharo image, you can execute the following script in Playground:

```
Metacello new
    baseline: 'Parasol';
    repository: 'github://SeasideSt/Parasol/repository';
    load: 'tests'.
```

Once this is done you can start

```
ZnZincServerAdaptor startOn: 8080.
```

Since Parasol uses Selenium WebDriver, you must download Selenium WebDriver and a browser driver, this last one depends on which browser you want to use to test your application.

Downloading Selenium web driver

Selenium server is a project that contains a set of tools and libraries that enable and support the automation of web browsers. Selenium is a Java program, therefore it requires a Java Runtime Environment (JRE) 1.6 or a new version to run it. If Java Runtime Environment (JRE) is not installed on your system, you can download the JRE from the Oracle website.

In this chapter, we use Selenium server 3.141.x to run our examples. You can download it from the official page of Selenium. The name of the file should contain the following prefix:

```
selenium-server-standalone-3.141.x.jar
```

You may use the following command to run Selenium server on your computer.

```
java -Dwebdriver.chrome.driver=chromedriver -jar
    selenium-server-standalone-3.141.x.jar
```

Note that for running the previous command you need to configure Java in the PATH (environment variable).

Browser driver

Selenium requires a driver to interact with the web browser. For instance, Chrome requires Chromedriver, which must be installed before the following examples can be run. The table below shows browsers compatible with Parasol and their respective links to download.

Browser Driver	URL
Chrome	https://sites.google.com/a/chromium.org/chromedriver/downloads
Firefox	https://github.com/mozilla/geckodriver/releases
Safari	https://webkit.org/blog/6900/webdriver-support-in-safari-10/

We use Chromedriver version 80.0.3987.106 to run the chapter examples, but you can use other browser drivers or another version that you want.

9.2 First steps with Selenium

This section describes a simple test written using Parasol. This section assumes that you have already installed Parasol and Selenium server is already running.

A first test

Let's start easy and assume we want to test if the title of the http://pharo.org website is correct. For this, first, we need to create a class that inherits from TestCase.

```
TestCase << #PharoOrgTest
    package: 'FT-Parasol'
```

Then, we create a method called testTitleOfPharoPage as follows:

```
PharoOrgTest >> testTitleOfPharoPage

    | driver |
    driver := BPRemoteWebDriver withCapabilities: BPChromeOptions new.
    driver get: 'https://pharo.org/'.
    self assert: 'Pharo - Welcome to Pharo!' equals: driver getTitle.
    driver close.
```

Step-by-step explanation

First, we create a subclass of TestCase, we do not need instance or class variables for now. We placed this subclass in the FT-Parasol package.

```
TestCase << #PharoOrgTest
    package: 'FT-Parasol'
```

The testTitleOfPharoPage method contains a temporary variable that we use to save our instance of the Chrome WebDriver.

```
| driver |
driver := BPRemoteWebDriver withCapabilities: BPChromeOptions new.
```

Note that if you want to use another driver, you must change the class BPChromeOptions to another browser driver compatible with Parasol.

The get method loads a given URL and allows you to navigate through the website. The WebDriver will wait until the page is fully loaded before returning the control to the test. If your page loads a large amount of AJAX, then WebDriver may not know when the page has been fully loaded.

```
driver get: 'https://pharo.org/'.
```

The next line of our method is an assertion to confirm that the title of the page is equal to: 'Pharo - Welcome to Pharo!'.

```
self assert: 'Pharo - Welcome to Pharo!' equals: driver getTitle.
```

Finally, we close the browser window.

```
driver close.
```

You may also use the method `quit` instead `close`. The difference is that `quit` will come out of the browser, and `close` will close a tab. Note that the `close` method will close a tab only if there is an open tab, by default most browsers will close completely.

Improve the structure of your test

In our previous example, we wrote the entire test in one method, however, the best practice is to add all the prerequisites of the tests on the `setUp` method and all the steps of cleaning on the `tearDown` method.

Therefore, to improve the structure of these tests, we first will convert the temporary variable driver into an instance variable.

```
TestCase << #PharoOrgTest
    slots: { #driver } ;
    package: 'FT-Parasol'
```

Next, we will place the statements that load the driver in the `setUp` method:

```
PharoOrgTest >> setUp
    super setUp.
    driver := BPRemoteWebDriver withCapabilities: BPChromeOptions new.
    driver get: 'https://pharo.org/'
```

In the same way, we move the cleaning statements in the `tearDown` method:

```
PharoOrgTest >> tearDown
    super tearDown.
    driver quit
```

Finally, our test method will be rewritten as follows:

```
PharoOrgTest >> testTitleOfPharoPage
    self assert: 'Pharo - Welcome to Pharo!' equals: driver getTitle.
```

Now, if you run this test again, you should behave in the same way as the first version of our test we saw.

9.3 Locating elements with Parasol: The basics

In our tests, we would like to verify also if some particular HTML elements display the information we want. But before performing this verification, we first need to find these elements. Parasol uses what are called *Locators* to find and match the elements of the web page. Parasol has eight locators as shown in the following table.

Locator	Example
ID	findElementByID: 'user'
Name	findElementByName: 'username'
Link Text	findElementByLinkText: 'Login'
Partial Link Text	findElementByPartialLinkText: 'Next'
XPath	findElementsByXPath: '//div[@id="login"]/input'
Tag Name	findElementsByTagName: 'body'
Class Name	findElementsByClassName: 'table'
CSS	findElementByCSSSelector: '#login > input[type="text"]'

You can use any of them to find the element that you are looking for in your application. The following paragraphs briefly describe how to use a number of these locators.

Find element by ID

The use of ID is the easiest and probably the safest way to locate an element in HTML. Test scripts that use IDs are less prone to changes in the application. For example, consider the following HTML form:

```
<form method="get">
    <input id="fullName" name="textInfo" type="text"/>
    <input id="submitButton" type="submit"/>
</form>
```

We may locate the input field by its ID, as follows:

```
textField := driver findElementByID: 'fullName'.
```

If no element has the ID attribute that matches the provided one, a BPNoSuchElementException exception will be raised.

Find element by name

An HTML element may have an attribute called *name*, they are normally used in the forms such as text fields and selection buttons. The values of the attributes of the name are passed to the server when a form is sent. In terms of a lower probability of change, the attribute name is probably the second in importance after ID.

Considering the previous HTML code example, you can locate the elements using the `findElementByName` method:

```
textField := driver findElementByName: 'textInfo'.
```

Find element by link and partial link

It is possible to find an element based on its link. You can use this way of the location of elements when you know the link text used inside of an anchor tag. With this strategy, the first element with the value of the text link that matches the location will be returned. For instance, we may find the following anchor element:

```
<a href="https://pharo.org/">Go to Pharo!</a>
```

The HTML element can be located in the following ways:

```
linkPharo := driver findElementByLinkText: 'Go to Pharo!'.
linkPharo := driver findElementByPartialLinkText: 'Go to'.
```

Notice that with `findElementByPartialLinkText` we don't need to give the full-text link, just part of it.

Find element by tag name

Finding elements by a tag name is used when you want to locate an element by the name of its label. However, because there is a limited set of tag names, it is very possible that more than one element with the same name of tag exists, so this locator is not normally used to identify an element, instead, it is more common to use it in chained locations.

Consider our previous example form:

```
<form method="get">
  <input id="inputField" name="textInfo" type="text"/>
  <input id="submitButton" type="submit"/>
</form>
```

We could locate the input element (input) as follows:

```
input := driver findElementByTagName: 'input'
```

Find element by class name

The class attribute of an HTML element is used to add style to our pages. And it can be used to identify elements too.

9.4 Finding elements using XPath

In the next example:

```
<p id="testParagraph" class="testclass1">Bla bla</p>
<a class="testclass2">foobar</a>
```

We can use any of the following lines to locate the *testclass* elements.

```
testClassOne := driver findElementByClassName: 'testclass1'.
testClassTwo := driver findElementByClassName: 'testclass2'.
```

It is common in web applications to use the same class attribute in several elements, so be careful if you try to get the elements by class name.

Find element by CSS selector

You can locate an element through the syntax of the CSS selector.

For example, the element p of the next HTML code:

```
<p class="content">Hello, how are you?</p>
```

It could be located like this:

```
paragraphHello := driver findElementByCSSSelector: 'p.content'
```

9.4 Finding elements using XPath

XPath, the XML Path Language, is a query language for selecting nodes from an XML document. When a browser renders a web page, the HTML contents may be parsed into a DOM tree or similar. Therefore, it is possible to find a specific node in the tree using XPath. To illustrate how to find an element with XPath, we will use the next HTML code as example:

```
    <div id="testDiv1">
  <p id="testDiv1p" class="c1"></p>
    </div>
    <div id="testDiv2">
  <p id="testDiv2p1" class="c2"></p>
  <p id="testDiv2p2" class="c1"></p>
  <p id="testDiv2p3" class="c1"></p>
    </div>
```

Imagine that we need to get the div with ID equal to testDiv2, so we use the next code snippet to get it:

```
testDiv := driver findElementByXPath: '//div[@id=''testDiv2'']'
```

For locating elements with XPath, we first need to understand their syntax. Therefore, to use this option, you will first need to learn XPath syntax.

Note that XPath is a very powerful way to locate web elements when by id, by name, or by link text are not applicable. However, XPath expressions are vulnerable to structure changes around the web element, because the path from the root to the target element may change.

9.5 Finding multiple elements

There are some cases in which you can have more than one element with the same attributes. This is the case of the following example: two div siblings have the same attributes.

```
<div id = "div1">
  <input type="checkbox" name = "same" value="on">Same checkbox in
    Div1</input>
</div>
<div id = "div2">
  <input type="checkbox" name = "same" value="on">Same checkbox in
    Div2</input>
</div>
```

Chaining findElement to find a child element

In these cases, XPATH can be used, however, there is a simpler way, using nested selectors which is nothing else than locating elements in the result of a previous location. For example, the following locates the div entry with id 'div2':

```
inputOfDiv2 := (driver findElementByID: 'div2') findElementByName:
    'same'
```

Multiple elements

As the name suggests, `findElementsByTagName` returns a list of matching elements. Its syntax is exactly the same as `findElement`, but in the plural `findElements`.

For example, to get all div of our previous example:

```
divElements := driver findElementsByTagName: 'div'.
```

Sometimes, findElement fails due to multiple matching elements on a page, of which one was not aware. findElements will be useful to find them.

9.6 Interacting with the elements

Until now we saw how to navigate through a URL and how to select elements. Now, our next step is to interact with these elements. You can do different things with these elements depending on their type. Using the following form as an example we will show how to interact with it and its elements.

```
<html>
<body>
<h1>Sign in</h1>
<form id="loginForm">
    <input name="username" type="text" />
    <input name="password" type="password" />
    <button name="login" type="submit" class= "btn
    btn-primary">Login</button>
    <a href="forgotPassworsd.html">Do you forgot your password?</a>
    <p class="content">
        "Are you new here?"
        <a href="register.html">Create an account</a>
    </p>
</form>
</body>
<html>
```

Filling text in a text field

To fill in the username and password fields in this form, we first have to select them, for this, we will use the following code:

```
name := driver findElementByName: 'username'.
password := driver findElementByName: 'password'
```

Now it is possible to fill text in these fields as follows:

```
name sendKeys: 'John'.
password sendKeys: 'xxxxxxx'.
```

It is possible to send the message `sendKeys:` in any element: This makes it possible to validate keyboard shortcuts. However, writing something in a text field does not automatically delete it. Instead, what you write will be attached to what is already there. You can easily delete the content of a text field or text area with the message `clear`.

Activating links and buttons

Another very useful action in the navigation of web pages is to click on links and buttons, such action is activated using the message `click` on the selected element. Below is an example of how to use it with our form.

```
loginButton := driver findElementByName: 'login'.
loginButton click.
```

9.7 Parasol in action

Previous sections introduced Parasol features through basic examples. This section applies everything learned during the chapter to create a number of tests for a small but real website called *Mercury Tours*. *Mercury Tours* is an agency that offers trips. Maybe if you worked with automated web tests before, you are familiar with them.

Setting up tests

First, we will create a subclass of test called `EPTest`:

```
TestCase << #EPTest
    slots: { #driver } ;
    package: 'Example-Parasol-Tests'
```

As we see in previous sections, the instance variable driver represents our browser driver necessary to work with Parasol and its methods. Second, we need to initialize the driver and load the page, since we need to do this step for all the tests we will place this in the `setUp` method.

```
EPTest >> setUp
    super setUp.
    driver := BPRemoteWebDriver withCapabilities: BPChromeOptions new.
    driver get: self baseURL

EPTest >> baseURL
    ^ 'http://newtours.demoaut.com/'
```

As you notice, we use `self baseURL` to get the URL. It is not necessary to separate the URL in a method.

Finally, we define the `tearDown` method:

```
EPTest >> tearDown
    driver quit.
    super tearDown
```

It is important to use the `quit` message to close the browser when a test ends, as we mentioned in second section of this chapter. With the `setUp` and `tearDown` method, we are able to do any test on the page.

9.8 Testing the page title

Our first test will verify if our URL is the principal URL of web page, which is defined as follows:

```
EPTest >> testPageEntry
  | title |
  title := driver getTitle.
  self assert: title equals: 'Welcome: Mercury Tours'
```

Remember that if we run Parasol tests we must first run the Selenium server. With the Selenium server and the test running, we can see that our browser was opened and can see the home of our tested page:

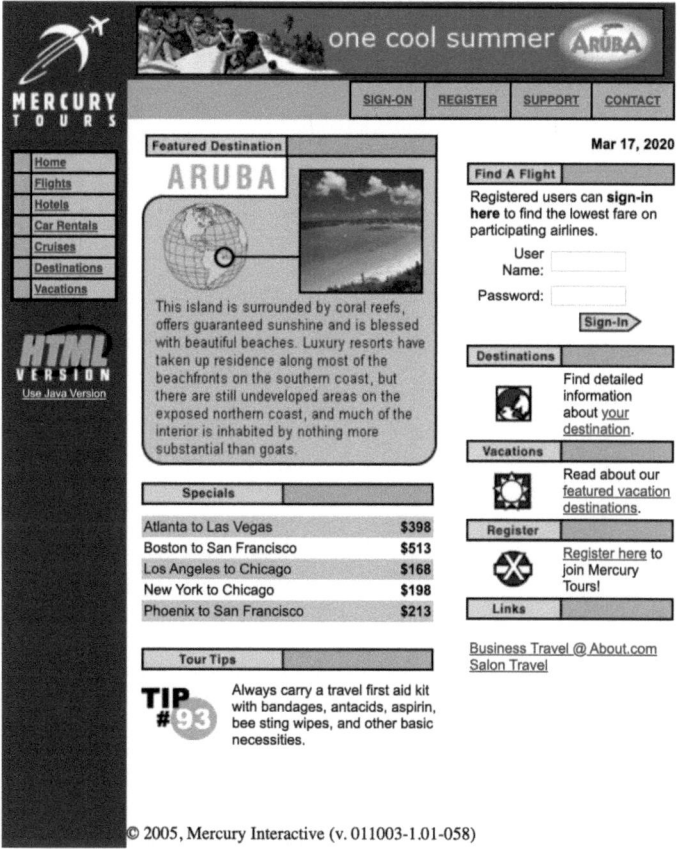

Figure 9-1 The Mercury Tours WebSite.

After the web browser is closed, we can see that the test passed because our page has the title *Welcome: Mercury Tours* in our tab. So it's time to do something more complex.

9.9 Testing displayed information

The Mercury Tours page has a lot of information on its home page. So, why not try to test this information? As an example, we will write a test to verify the information in the table called *specials*. Assume that you want to test that the first row is the flight from Atlanta to Las Vegas and the price is $398. How do we do that? The first step is to know how our page represents this information.

Use the developer tools of Chrome browser and select the desired row. We get the following HTML code:

```
<tr bgcolor="#CCCCCC">
    <td width="80%">
    <font face="Arial, Helvetica, sans-serif, Verdana" size="2">
        Atlanta to Las Vegas
    </font>
    </td>
    <td width="20%">
    <div align="right">
    <font face="Arial, Helvetica, sans-serif, Verdana" size="2">
        <b>$398</b>
    </font>
    </div>
    </td>
</tr>
```

We can see the following details:

- The row is inside a table.
- The table or the row does not contain an ID or a Class that we can use to find this element.
- The CSS or the Tag Name can't help us to find this row.

In this special case, XPath is a useful locator in this particular case. First, we need to create a subclass of `EPTest`. We are using `EPTest` as a base class for future test classes. This decision gives us a number of benefits, for instance, we may find easily all test classes by inspecting the subclasses of `EPTest`, and we can reuse some methods in the subclasses, in particular, the `setUp` and `tearDown` methods.

Therefore, we define the following class:

9.9 Testing displayed information

```
EPTest << #EPHomePageTest
  package: 'Example-Parasol-Tests'
```

`EPHomePageTest` is a class only dedicated to testing the home page and all elements that are part of this. Taking our HTML code as a base, create a method to get the flight and its price, then test if the value of these elements is the same as the expected result. The following method gives us the expected result, but it contains some things that we can improve.

```
EPHomePageTest >> testPriceAndInfoForFlightFromAtlantaToLasVegas

self assert: ((driver findElementByXPath:
    '/html/body/div/table/tbody/tr/td[2]/table/tbody/
tr[4]/td/table/tbody/tr/td[2]/table/tbody/tr[2]/td[1]/
table[1]/tbody/tr[3]/td/table/tbody/tr[1]/td[1]/font') getText)
    equals: 'Atlanta to Las Vegas'.
self assert: ((driver findElementByXPath:
    '/html/body/div/table/tbody/tr/td[2]/table/tbody/tr[4]/td/table/tbody/tr/td[2]/
tr[2]/td[1]/table[1]/tbody/tr[3]/td/table/tbody/tr[1]/
td[2]/div/font/b') getText)
    equals: '$398'
```

We will refactor this method to make it more understandable. We will add a method to get the controller element.

```
EPHomePageTest >> descriptionFlightFromAtlantaToLasVegas
    ^ driver findElementByXPath: '/html/body/div/table/tbody/tr/td[2]/
    table/tbody/tr[4]/td/table/tbody/tr/td[2]/table/tbody/tr[2]/td[1]/
    table[1]/tbody/tr[3]/td/table/tbody/tr[1]/td[1]/font'

EPHomePageTest >> priceFlightFromAtlantaToLasVegas
    ^ driver findElementByXPath: '/html/body/div/table/tbody/tr/td[2]/
    table/tbody/tr[4]/td/table/tbody/tr/td[2]/table/tbody/tr[2]/
    td[1]/table[1]/tbody/tr[3]/td/table/tbody/tr[1]/td[2]/div/font/b'
```

Then, we may now refactor the test method as follows:

```
EPHomePageTest >> testFlightFromAtlantaToLasVegas
    self
        assert: self descriptionFlightFromAtlantaToLasVegas getText
        equals: 'Atlanta to Las Vegas'.
    self
        assert: self priceFlightFromAtlantaToLasVegas getText
        equals: '$398'
```

We test a part of the home page, if you want to test other parts, follow the previous steps and try to construct multiple tests. The tests above are a good example of how we get elements from an HTML page and test if the displayed page contains the correct information we want to display.

9.10 Testing interactions

We will now show how to test interactions. It's an important step to test, so we will explain how you could do it. In this example, we will create a test that registers a user on the website. First, we will create another subclass of `EPTest` called `EPRegisterUserTest`.

```
EPTest << #EPRegisterUserTest
  package: 'Example-Parasol-Tests'
```

In this website to register a user we need first click the REGISTER button in the bar menu. Therefore, we will create a method that emulates a click in the REGISTER button.

```
EPRegisterUserTest >> clickInRegisterButton
  (driver findElementByLinkText: 'REGISTER') click
```

We use this method in our `setUp` method as follows:

```
EPRegisterUserTest >> setUp
  super setUp.
  self clickInRegisterButton
```

With this little change, the first step that each test will perform is to move to the REGISTER form. You may see the REGISTER form in Figure 9-2.

Now, we are prepared to create tests in `EPRegisterUserTest`. Our first test is to verify if we are in the correct page when we click on the register button. So, create the test.

```
EPRegisterUserTest >> testEntryToRegisterPage
  | title |
  title := driver getTitle.
  self assert: title equals: 'Register: Mercury Tours'
```

In this page, we have a registration form with multiple fields. If we want to register on the page we must complete three sections in the form. Contact, mailing, and user information, so we define three tests to complete these sections.

As you remember, the first step is to see how the page renders the elements in the form. For this, we inspect the HTML code using the browser tools. The following code shows the contact information HTML code:

```
<tr>
<td align=right>
<font face="Arial, Helvetica, sans-serif" size="2">
<b>First Name: </b>
</font>
</td>
<td>
```

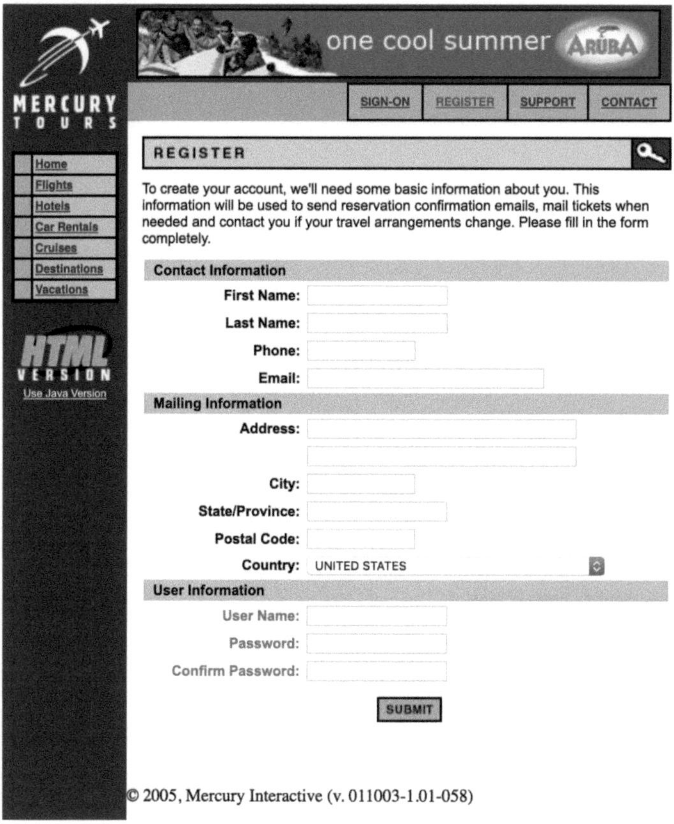

9.10 Testing interactions

Figure 9-2 Registration From

```
<input maxlength=60 name="firstName" size="20">
</td>
</tr>
 <tr>
 <td align=right>
 <font face="Arial, Helvetica, sans-serif" size="2">
 <b>Last Name: </b>
 </font>
 </td>
 <td>
 <input maxlength=60 name="lastName" size="20">
 </td>
</tr>
<tr>
```

```
<td align=right>
<font face="Arial, Helvetica, sans-serif" size="2">
<b>Phone:</b>
</font>
</td>
<td>
<input maxlength="20" name="phone" size="15">
</td>
</tr>
<tr>
<td align=right>
<font face="Arial, Helvetica, sans-serif" size="2">
<b>Email:</b>
</font>
</td>
<td>
<input name="userName" id="userName" size="35" maxlength="64">
</td>
</tr>
```

We can draw the following conclusions from the HTML code:

- All inputs have a name or an ID.
- All forms are in a table.

With these conclusions, we can start with the tests. The test `firstNameField` tests whether the correct information is entered into the contact information section. Like our previous methods, we need to create multiple methods to get the field's elements to put some information into them. In the following, we show one method that returns the field with the name `firstName`.

```
EPRegisterUserTest >> firstNameField
    ^ driver findElementByName: 'firstName'
```

You need to create as many of these as you need to get all the form fields you need for your test. The next step is to create a method to set information to fields. We use the message `sendKeys` to set the information that we want.

```
EPRegisterUserTest >> fillInformationToContactSection
    self firstNameField sendKeys: 'Jhon'.
    self lastNameField sendKeys: 'Stuart'.
    self phoneField sendKeys: '10276123'.
    self emailField sendKeys: 'example@mail.com'
```

Finally, we create the following test to verify if the introduced information is the same as the fields.

9.10 Testing interactions

```
EPRegisterUserTest >> testIntroduceInformationInContactSection
  self fillInformationToContactSection.
  self assert: (self firstNameField getAttribute: 'value') equals:
    'Jhon'.
  self assert: (self lastNameField getAttribute: 'value') equals:
    'Stuart'.
  self assert: (self phoneField getAttribute: 'value') equals:
    '10276123'.
  self assert: (self emailField getAttribute: 'value') equals:
    'example@mail.com'
```

If we run the test we can see how Parasol introduces the information to the fields (see Figure 9-3).

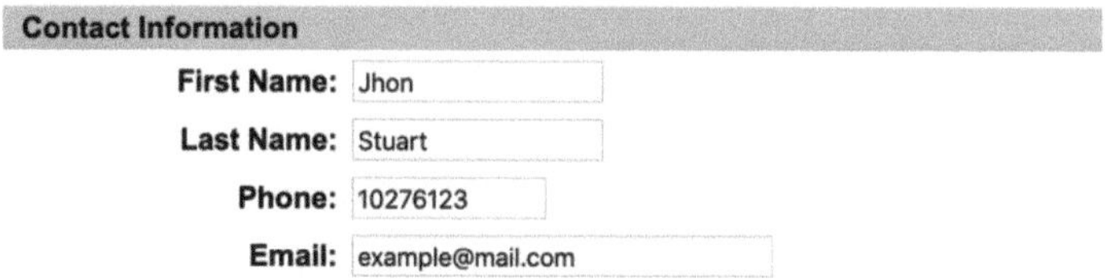

Figure 9-3 Filling fields using Parasol.

Now, we can create tests to fill in the information to other sections. An important observation is the select box in the mailing information section. If we want to test it, we need to use another method to assert it. In this case, the selected option contains the attribute called `selected`. So, we define the next method to get this element:

```
EPRegisterUserTest >> getSelectedOfCountry
  (self countryField findElementsByTagName: 'option') do: [ :each |
    (each getAttribute: 'selected')
      ifNotNil: [ ^ each ] ]
```

When you create the test, with this method you only get the element that contain the information that we need. So we use the `getText` message and assert if the fields contain the correct information.

```
EPRegisterUserTest >> testIntroduceInformationInMailingSection
  self assert: (self getSelectedOfCountry getText) equals: 'UNITED
    STATES '.
```

It is also possible to change the value of the combo box using the sendKeys message as we saw in previous examples.

Now, with all fields tested, we define a test for the user registration on the page. If you created the `fillInformationToMailingSection` and `fill-`

InformationToUserSection methods, we will use these methods. If you didn't, you need to create these methods.

We need another method to find the submit button and click it, so we create it.

```
EPRegisterUserTest >> clickInSubmitButton
    (driver findElementByName: 'register') click
```

In the page, when you register a user you obtain the following view:

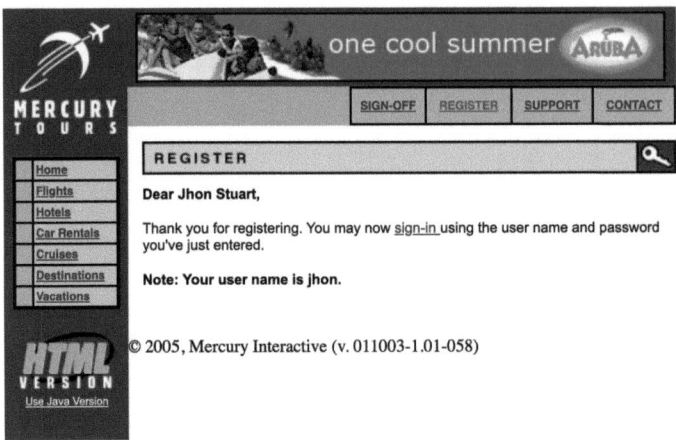

Figure 9-4 Registration successful view.

We have two options to assert if the user is registered:

- Get the text 'sign-off' of the sign-off option
- Get the description text below the register title.

You can use any of these options, as an example we will get the description text. So define the method to find the description text.

```
EPRegisterUserTest >> descriptionText
    ^ driver findElementByXPath: '/html/body/div/table/tbody/tr/td[2]/table/tbody/tr[4]/td/table/tbody/tr/td[2]/table/tbody/tr[3]/td/p[2]/font'
```

And finally create the test to verify if the user is registered successfully.

```
EPRegisterUserTest >> testRegistrationOfUser
    <timeout: 10>
    self sendInformationToContactSection.
    self sendInformationToMailingSection.
    self sendInformationToUserSection.
    self clickInSubmitButton.
```

```
    self
        assert: (self descriptionText getText)
        equals: 'Thank you for registering.
You may now sign-in using the user name
and password you''ve just entered.'
```

Sometimes this test can fail because the page needs to save the new user and load the successful message. Another problem that can cause the test failure is the time it takes for our Selenium server to use the browser driver. So we use the timeout pragma to try to avoid this, but you can also use the `Delay` class. If you don't have this problem, delete the line.

Finally, run the test and observe its result. If the test passed, you are now able to create multiple tests using Parasol.

9.11 Conclusion

The purpose of this chapter was to introduce the basics of Parasol to create a test suite. You should now be able to find elements in a website, fill in the information in fields, and interact with the website through links and buttons.

CHAPTER 10

MockObject and Teachable: Two simple mocking approaches

Imagine that you want to test a network protocol, you do now want to rely on a real network but you would like to fix certain parameters and make that your protocol is reacting correctly. You can use *mock* objects to represent a part of the world during your tests. A mock object is an object that supports testing in isolation and represents a behavior that should be fixed from a test point of view.

There are several frameworks for defining mock objects: BabyMock and Mocketry are two of the most sophisticated. In this chapter, we present two super simple and minimalist mocking approaches. We start with an extension that has been introduced as an extension of SUnit in Pharo 9. Its implementation is simple and available in the package SUnit-MockObjects. It has been designed by Giovanni Corriga.

10.1 About MockObject design

While simpler and less sophisticated than other libraries, this implementation is still quite powerful. This implementation takes a different approach compared to BabyMock/BabyMock2 and Mocketry:

- there are no methods such as `should`, `can`, or `be:`,
- the mocks are stricter in their behavior – users need to send all and only the defined messages, in the same order as they were defined.

- the mocks need to be manually verified using the new message `TestCase>>verify:` defined on `TestCase`.

These limitations are on purpose, mainly for two reasons:

- to discourage the use of these objects unless they are really needed.
- to keep the implementation simple so that it can be integrated into Pharo's SUnit library, as opposed to being its own framework.

This extension is similar to Pharo Teachable that you can find at: https://github.com/astares/Pharo-Teachable and that we present below as an addition.

10.2 MockObject

I am a test double object that can be used as a stub, a fake, or a mock. I provide a simple protocol so that the user can teach me what messages to expect, and how to behave or respond to these messages.

Usage

A new object can be created with `MockObject new`, or using the utility methods on the class side 'instance creation' protocol.

The main message to teach a MockObject is `on:withArguments:verify:`; the other methods in the 'teaching' protocol all use this message. This message takes a selector symbol, a collection of arguments, and a block. By sending this message, the mock object is trained to evaluate the block when receiving a message matching the selector and the arguments.

Other variations of this message have more specialized behavior:

- `on:withArguments:respond:` will simply return its third argument when the mock receives a matching message;
- likewise `on:withArguments:` will return the mock itself.

The other methods in the 'teaching' protocol provide an ergonomic API for this behavior.

A mock object will expect to receive only the messages it has been trained on, in the same order and number as it was trained. If it receives an unknown message or a known message but in the wrong order, it will simply return itself.

10.3 Stubs, Fakes, and Mocks

A MockObject can be used as a stub by not using the `verify:` variants of the 'teaching' protocol.

To use the MockObject as a real mock, the user needs to verify its use. This is done by means of the `TestCase>>verify:` message. Verification needs to be triggered by the user - it's not automatic.

The `verify:` message will assert

- that the mock has received all the messages it has been trained on,
- that it has not received only those messages, and
- that it has received the messages it has been trained on.

10.4 Example

We create a simple class named: `MyClassUsingMock` to use a mock.

```
TestCase << #MyClassUsingMock
  slots: { #mock };
  package: 'SUnit-MockObjects-Tests'
```

We create a mock object and teach it two messages `meaningOfLife` and `secondMeaning` that should be sent one after the other.

```
MyClassUsingMock >> setUp
  super setUp.
  mock := MockObject new.
  mock
    on: #meaningOfLife
    respond: 42.
  mock
    on: #secondMeaning
    respond: 84.
```

Then we can write a test that will send the message to the object and expect a given result. We can also verify that all the messages have been sent.

```
MyClassUsingMock >> testVerifyChecksThatAllTheMessageGotSent
  self assert: mock meaningOfLife equals: 42.
  self assert: mock secondMeaning equals: 84.
  self verify: mock
```

We can also specify which precise argument a message should be passed using the message `on:with:respond:` or `on:with:with:respond:`.

```
MyClassUsingMock2 >> setUp
  super setUp.
  mock := MockObject new.
  mock
    on: #meaningOfLife:
    with: 22
    respond: 42.
  mock
    on: #secondMeaning:and:
    with: 32
    with: 64
    respond: 84.
```

The following test checks that a mock is not returning a correct answer.

```
MyClassUsingMock2 >> testMeaningOfLifeDoesNotPassCorrectValue
  self
    should: [ self assert: (mock meaningOfLife: 33) equals: 42]
    raise: TestFailure
```

The following one checks that the mock object returns the correct answers.

```
MyClassUsingMock2 >> testMeaningOfLife
  self assert: (mock meaningOfLife: 22) equals: 42.
  self assert: (mock secondMeaning: 32 and: 64) equals: 84
```

10.5 About matching arguments

Regarding the arguments matching, the code always goes through the matching logic but it's still quite flexible. The following three possibilities are supported:

- ignoring the arguments: if the message send has no arguments of interest,
- full match: if all arguments of the actual message send match the expected arguments,
- partial match: the user of the mock should use `MockObject class>>any` for any argument that can be ignored. This is a special wildcard object to be used when we don't care about an argument.

For example, let's assume we have this code under test:

```
aMock messageToBeMocked: 1 withArguments: 'two'
```

This can be mocked in the three following ways: ignoring arguments, full match, or partial match.

10.6 Teachable

Ignoring arguments.
```
aMock on: #messageToBeMocked:withArguments:
```

Full match.
```
aMock
  on: #messageToBeMocked:withArguments:
  with: 1
  with: 'two'
```

Partial match.
```
aMock
  on: #messageToBeMocked:withArguments:
  with: MockObject any
  with: 'two'
```

The above training methods are to be used when we don't care about the behavior when mocking, but only when the message is sent. If we want to control what is returned by the message send, we can use the `respond:` variants. If we want even finer control e.g. side effects, raising exceptions we can use the `verify:` variants.

10.6 Teachable

The other simple library for mocking objects is Pharo Teachable. It is not integrated into SUnit but still worth checking it. It is developed by Torsten Bergman.

Installation

You can install Teachable using the following expression:

```
Metacello new
  repository: 'github://astares/Pharo-Teachable/src';
  baseline: 'Teachable';
  load
```

Teachable is a class whose instances can be taught to respond to messages. It's useful for creating mocks that should behave like other objects (for instance inside of a test case) without actually implementing a real mock class.

Here is an example of how it can be used:

```
| teachable |
teachable := Teachable new.
teachable
    whenSend: #help return: 'ok';
    whenSend: #doit evaluate: [ 1 inspect ];
    acceptSend: #noDebugger;
    whenSend: #negate: evaluate: [ :num | num negated ].
```

After teaching the object we can use it as if it had a normal implementation in a class:

```
teachable help.
  "this will return the string 'ok'"
teachable doit.
  "this will open the inspector on the SmallInteger 1"
teachable noDebugger.
  "this will accept the send of #noDebugger and return the teachable"
teachable negate: 120
  "this will return -120"
```

10.7 Conclusion

We presented two little approaches to support simple mock objects by providing a way to teach values or actions to be performed by the mock. More mature and powerful frameworks exist: BabyMock and Mocketry.

CHAPTER 11

Performance testing with SMark

Measuring performance is not an easy activity. It involves many considerations that you need to take into account such as the pertinence of what you want to measure, how you can isolate it from other computations, ... Indeed an execution may be affected by different factors, for instance, the hardware you have, the VM you are using, the run-time optimizations that the VM perform while your program is running, the unpredictable garbage collection, among many others. All these factors combined make it difficult to have a good estimation of the performance of an execution.

This chapter introduces SMark, a testing framework for benchmarking Pharo applications. SMark is developed and maintained by Stephan Marr. SMark encapsulates a number of benchmarking best practices that are useful to take into account these factors and help us to have a decent execution time estimation.

11.1 Installing SMark

You can install SMark with the following code snippet:

```
Metacello new
    baseline: 'SMark';
    repository: 'github://smarr/SMark';
    load.
```

The examples in this chapter were performed in Pharo 8.

11.2 Measuring execution time

Measuring execution time needs to be done carefully, otherwise, we can get a very far estimation of it. To illustrate the extent of this situation, we will use the recursive Fibonacci function as a subject under analysis. Define a new class named Math and the following method:

```
Math >> fib: n
   ^n <= 1
     ifTrue: [ n ]
     ifFalse: [ (self fib: (n - 1)) + (self fib: (n - 2)) ]
```

We now will measure how many seconds take to compute the 40th Fibonacci, using the message timeToRun method of the BlockClosure class as follows:

```
[ [ Math new fib: 40 ] timeToRun
```

The method timeToRun basically records the system clock time before and after the execution of the code block. We execute this script 5 times, you may find the results of each execution in the following lines:

```
1 execution: 1091 milliseconds
2 execution: 1046 milliseconds
3 execution: 1098 milliseconds
4 execution: 1069 milliseconds
5 execution: 1085 milliseconds
```

As you can see, even in this small example, there is a variation between the results in the five iterations. Even though the measurements were done on the same computer, in the same Pharo Image. What happened? As we mentioned in the introduction the VM and the Hardware perform plenty of activities at the moment to execute a piece of code, and some of these activities are not deterministic, for instance, without going too far, some collections like the class Set that save objects without a defined (or let say, deterministic) order.

For this reason, it is necessary to consider a number of good practices to measure execution time, and minimize the measurement bias and uncertainty. For instance, execute the benchmarks a number of times before starting our measurements to let the VM perform the dynamic optimizations. Another recommendation is to execute multiple times the benchmark, use the media as a point of reference, and consider the error margin. These recommendations may vary depending on the VM you are using, and the characteristics of your benchmark. For instance, it is well known that time measurements have more variations in micro-benchmarks than macro-benchmarks.

But, don't worry, SMark takes many of these recommendations into account to help you in executing your benchmarks and get a decent execution time estimation.

11.3 A first benchmark in SMark

SMark has been designed to run benchmarks in a similar fashion to we run tests. Therefore, their creation is quite similar too. First, we need to create a subclass of the class SMarkSuite.

```
SMarkSuite << #MyBenchSuite
    package: 'SMark-Demo'
```

Then, we need to write the piece of code in which we are interested to measure the execution time (the benchmark), in our case, we will use our Fibonacci benchmark that we introduced in the previous section.

```
MyBenchSuite >> benchFib40
    self fib: 40.
```

To execute our benchmark, we only need to execute the following script in a playground.

```
MyBenchSuite runOnly: #benchFib40
```

If you print the script answer it shows a small report like this one:

```
Report for: MyBenchSuite
Benchmark Fib40
Fib40 total: iterations=1 runtime: 1099ms
```

As you can see, the execution time is similar to the ones we got in the previous section, but now we can use SMark to execute multiple times the benchmark and get a better time estimation.

```
MyBenchSuite runOnly:#benchFib40 iterations: 25
```

And we got the following report:

```
Report for: MyBenchSuite
Benchmark Fib40
Fib40 total: iterations=25 runtime: 1022.7ms +/-1.5
```

There you go, now we have the average execution time and error margin, the error margin measured with a 90% confidence degree assuming that the variable distribution is normal.

11.4 Setup and teardown

Similarly to SUnit, SMark offers two hook methods to define the actions to be done before and after a benchmark is executed.

11.5 SMark benchmark runners

The way that SMark will run benchmarks depends on the Smark runner you use. There are five different runners:

- SMarkRunner
- SMarkAutosizeRunner,
- SMarkCogRunner,
- SMarkProfileRunner, and
- SMarkWeakScalingRunner.

Each runner provides a particular way to perform the benchmarks. You may specify which runner you want to use by overriding the following method.

```
SMarkSuite class >> defaultRunner
    ^self onCog: [ SMarkCogRunner ] else: [ SMarkRunner ]
```

The message `defaultRunner` returns a CogRunner or a normal Runner depending on the VM on which the benchmark is executed. The next subsection describes each one of these runners.

SMarkRunner. It is the standard way to run a benchmark provided by SMark. SMarkRunner only performs the benchmark N times, where N is the number of iterations defined by the user, as we saw in the previous section. It records the time measurements of each execution to build a report.

SMarkCogRunner. It adds warning up instructions before executing the benchmark. SMarkCogRunner executes a benchmark twice before taking the measurements. The first execution is to execute the inline cache optimization done by the VM. The second execution is to trigger the JIT compiler to produce code. Once these two executions are performed the benchmark is executed N times similarly as SMarkRunner does.

SMarkAutosizeRunner. It increases the execution time of the benchmark to reach a target time, this is used mostly with micro-benchmarks. The default target time is 300 milliseconds. Therefore, if a benchmark takes less than 300 milliseconds to run, this runner will measure how many times this benchmark needs to be executed to meet the target time. Once the benchmark execution time meets the target time, this runner executes this increased benchmark N iterations to take the time measurements similar to SMarkRunner.

SMarkProfileRunner. It automatically opens and uses Pharo standard time profiler to monitor the execution of all the benchmarks in the suite. Then, the time profilers show the call context tree of this execution reporting which methods were executed by the benchmarks, and how much time each method consumes.

SMarkWeakScallingRunner. It is specific to platforms with support for real parallelism. Weak scaling is defined as how the solution time varies with the number of processors for a fixed problem size per processor.

11.6 Benchmark suites

Having a good benchmark already packaged and identified is important to be able to compare changes for example in the compiler or other aspects of execution. SMark provides four benchmarks suites:

- *SMarkCompiler*, a benchmark that measures the time needed to compile a regular-size method.
- *SMarkLoops*, a set of microbenchmarks measuring a number of basic aspects such as message send, instance field access, and array access cost.
- *SMarkSlopstone*, a Smalltalk Low-level OPeration Stones Portable Low-Level Benchmarks for ST80 and ST/V (using 16-bit SmallIntegers) - Placed in public domain January 1993 (c) Bruce Samuelson Permission is given to place this in public Smalltalk archives.
- *SMarkSmopstone*, a Smalltalk Medium level OPeration Stones Portable Medium level Benchmarks for ST80 and ST/V (using 16-bit SmallInts) Placed in public domain January 1993 (c) Bruce Samuelson Permission is given to place this in public Smalltalk archives.

You may run any of these benchmark suites by performing the class method run of any of the previous classes. For instance:

```
SMarkLoops run
```

11.7 Result reports

SMark provides an option to export the benchmarking results using the class SMarkSimpleStatisticsReporter. For instance, consider the following example:

```
| stream result textReport|
result := SMarkLoops run.
stream := TextStream on: String new.
SMarkSimpleStatisticsReporter reportFor: result on: stream.
testReport := stream contents.
```

It runs the benchmark suite SMarkLoops and uses the class `SMarkSimpleStatisticsReporter` to export the results in a stream, in this particular case on a TextStream. This report is particularly useful to integrate SMark in a continuous integration environment.

11.8 Conclusion

This chapter introduces SMark, a framework to help you define, execute and report your benchmarks. It provides different ways to run your benchmarks, collect the results, and perform a simple statistical analysis to measure the error margin. In addition, SMark provides four benchmark suites that are useful to test the performance of a number of core functionalities in Pharo.